26 Ways

To Make

Money

Online

Financial Growth
Passive Income
Online Profits

Book 1

Milena Sladkova

First paperback edition: January 2024
Cover: Milena Sladkova

Disclaimer: The contents of this book are for informational purposes only and are not intended to provide legal, financial, or professional advice. The information provided is based on author's personal experience and research and should not be relied upon as a substitute for professional advice. Readers are encouraged to consult with a qualified professional regarding their specific circumstances before making any decisions. All the information and strategies presented in this book are accurate to the best of the author's knowledge at the time of writing. However, the online landscape is dynamic and subject to constant change. Laws, regulations, and online platforms can evolve, and what may have been effective or accurate at the time of writing may no longer be so in the future. The author and publisher disclaim any liability arising directly or indirectly from the use of the information in this book.

Table of contents (Book 1):

To be continued in Book 2: 27 Additional Way To Make Money Online

Introduction

In an era where the digital landscape continually expands, opportunities to make money online have become more accessible than ever before. Whether you're seeking to supplement your income or embark on a part-time online career, "*26 Ways To Make Money Online*" is your comprehensive guide to navigating the ever-evolving world of online income possibilities.

Within the pages of Book 1, you'll discover a diverse array of online *money-making strategies*, each outlined in its own dedicated chapter. From harnessing the power of **stock photography** to creating **viral websites**, my aim is to present you with a spectrum of options, allowing you to choose the path that best aligns with your interests, skills, and aspirations.

Before we explore the specifics of each method, it's essential to acknowledge that success in the online realm doesn't come overnight. It requires dedication, adaptability, and a willingness to stay informed about the latest trends and developments. The digital world is a dynamic place. Online platforms, algorithms, and consumer behavior evolve, and what works today might require adjustments tomorrow.

The strategies presented in this book are not one-size-fits-all solutions. Your journey to *online success* will be uniquely yours, shaped by your individual experiences, the effort you invest, and the skills you have and are willing to learn. This book is intended as an *informational resource* to inspire and guide you on your quest for online financial independence.

As you explore the chapters within, I encourage you to approach each opportunity with an open mind and a willingness to learn. Whether you're drawn to the artistic possibilities of *AI art*, the entrepreneurial spirit of *dropshipping*, or the communicative power of *writing*, there is a path that can lead you toward your online income goals.

And stay tuned for <u>Book 2</u>, where we will dive even deeper into the world of *online income generation*. In <u>Book 2</u>, we will explore **27 additional methods** to make money online, including *Amazon FBA*, *proofreading*, *publishing a book on KDP*, and many more. Together, these two books will provide you with a comprehensive toolkit for navigating the digital landscape and seizing the opportunities it offers.

Without further ado, let's embark on this digital journey together. "<u>*26 Ways To Make Money Online*</u>" is here to guide you through the process.

The digital frontier is vast, and your potential for success is limited only by your determination, creativity, and the effort you're willing to put forth. It's time to turn the virtual realm into your playground for **financial growth**. Let's begin.

#1

Stock Photography

Capturing Profits

Stock photography sites are online platforms where photographers can upload and sell their photographs to individuals and businesses for use in various projects such as advertising, websites, and publications. These sites allow photographers to make their work available to a wide audience, increasing the potential for sales and *earning revenue*. The earning potential for photographers on stock photography sites can vary widely, depending on factors such as the quality and popularity of their work, the commission rate of the site, and the number of sales they are able to make. Some successful photographers are able to earn a *full-time income* from stock photography, while others may earn a more modest supplementary income.

The good news are that stock photography sites are not only for photographers. While photographers are the main contributors of content on these sites, other creative professionals such as *graphic designers* and *illustrators* may also upload and sell their work. Many stock photography sites also offer a variety of other types of digital assets such as video footage, audio clips, and 3D models, which can be purchased and used in a variety of projects. Stock photography sites offer a platform for businesses and individuals to purchase and license stock content, making it a convenient and cost-effective way to access a wide range of creative assets.

Skillset

To be successful as a contributor on a stock photography site, there are a few skills that are important to have:

1.   *Photography skills*: As a photographer, you will need to have a good understanding of composition, lighting, and camera settings in order to produce high-quality images that will sell well on the site.

2.   *Post-processing skills*: You will also need to have good skills in editing software such as Adobe Lightroom or Photoshop to process and enhance your images.

3.   *Business skills*: Selling your work on a stock photography site is a business and having a good understanding of how to market your work effectively and manage your finances can help you succeed.

4.   *Understanding of the stock photography industry*: Familiarizing yourself with what sells well on stock photography sites, understanding the legal requirements and terms of the industry can help you to make the most of your stock photography business.

5.   *Adaptability*: With the industry and technology constantly changing, it's important to be able to adapt and stay current with the latest trends and technologies to stay competitive.

If you are not a photographer, but still want to contribute to stock photography sites, you will need the same skills but related to the *type of content* you are contributing.

The process of getting started

If you're interested in getting started with selling your work on a stock photography site, here are a few steps you can take:

1.   *Build a portfolio*: Start by building a strong portfolio of your best work that showcases your skills and style. Make sure that your images are well-composed, well-lit, and of high quality.

2.   *Research stock photography sites*: Look into different stock photography sites and compare their commission rates, terms, and the type of content they feature. Some sites may specialize in certain types of content such as travel photography or illustrations, while others may have a more general focus.

3.   *Sign up as a contributor*: Once you've chosen a stock photography site, sign up as a contributor and upload your portfolio. You will typically need to provide some basic information about yourself and your work, and may need to pass a review process before your work can be made available for sale.

4.   *Optimize your images for search*: Make sure to properly title, describe, and tag your images so that they will be easily found by potential customers. Check out how to simplify this process and add keywords to your images using AI Tools on page 41.

5.   *Promote your work*: Use social media and other online platforms to promote your work and build a following. Share your images on Instagram, Twitter, and other platforms, and consider creating a website or blog to showcase your work.

6.   *Track your sales and earnings, and adjust your strategy accordingly*: Keep track of the sales and earnings of your images, so you can adjust your strategy to optimize your earning potential.

Stock photography is a business, so it takes time and effort to build a successful portfolio and generate sales. But with persistence and hard work, you can build a sustainable income as a stock photographer.

Investment

The amount of time and money that you will need to invest to get started with selling your work on a stock photography site can vary depending on your current level of experience and equipment.

In terms of time, you will need to invest time in building your portfolio, researching stock photography sites, and optimizing your images for search. You will also need to spend time promoting your work and building a following.

In terms of money, you will need to invest in equipment and editing software. If you are already a professional photographer, you may already have the equipment you need to get started. If you are just starting out, you will need to invest in a camera, lenses, and editing software such as Adobe Lightroom or Photoshop.

Equipment on a budget

If you're on a budget and looking to get started with *stock photography*, there are a few pieces of equipment that you can consider investing in:

1.   *Camera*: You can find entry-level DSLR or mirrorless cameras at reasonable prices. Some popular options in the budget range include the Canon EOS Rebel T7 or the Nikon D3500.

2.   *Lens*: A basic 50mm lens is a great starting point as it is versatile and can be used for a variety of different types of photography. For example, the Canon EF 50mm f/1.8 STM lens or the Nikon 50mm f/1.8G lens are both budget-friendly options.

3.   *Tripod*: A good tripod is essential for keeping your camera steady and getting sharp images. You can find budget-friendly options such as the Manfrotto MT055CXPRO4 055 Tripod or the Joby GorillaPod 3K Kit.

4.   *Editing software*: Adobe Lightroom and Photoshop are industry-standard editing software, but they are not free. You can find some free alternatives such as GIMP or Lightzone.

You don't need to have the most expensive equipment to start selling your work on a stock photography site. With a bit of creativity and skill, you can produce high-quality images with even the most basic equipment.

Stock websites

There are many stock photography websites where you can become a contributor and sell your work. Some popular options include:

1.   **Shutterstock**: One of the largest and most well-known stock photography sites, with a wide variety of content including photos, illustrations, and videos. https://submit.shutterstock.com/

2.   **iStock** by **Getty Images**: A popular site with a large customer base, iStock offers a wide variety of content and also offers exclusive content for its customers. You have to use their app to become a contributor. https://www.istockphoto.com

3.   **Adobe Stock**: Adobe Stock is a stock photography site that is integrated with Adobe Creative Cloud, allowing users to search, license and manage images directly from within the Adobe Creative Suite. https://stock.adobe.com/contributor

4.   **Alamy**: Alamy is a stock photography site that specializes in editorial and commercial imagery, with a particular focus on news and events. https://www.alamy.com/become-a-contributor.aspx

5.   **Dreamstime**: Dreamstime is a stock photography site that offers a wide variety of content including photos, illustrations, and videos. They have a large customer base, and they also offer a referral program for contributors. https://www.dreamstime.com/sell-stock-photos-images

6.   **Depositphotos**: Depositphotos is a stock photography site that offers a wide variety of content and also offers exclusive content for their customers. https://contributors.depositphotos.com/

These are few examples of websites where you can become a contributor, and there are many other options available as well. Research different sites and determine which one is the best fit for your work.

Uploading the same files to multiple sites

It is generally recommended that you upload different files to different stock photography websites. Each site has its own guidelines and requirements for file size, resolution, and format, and uploading the same files to multiple sites can lead to rejection or other issues. <u>Some sites have exclusive content agreements with photographers, meaning that the content can only be sold through that specific platform.</u>

Some websites have a non-exclusive agreement, meaning you can submit the same images to other stock photography sites as well. That way you increase your earning potential by having your images available for purchase on different platforms.

Example: Images that are uploaded (and accepted) to Adobe Stock cannot be uploaded to any other platform.

Carefully read and understand the guidelines and requirements for each site before uploading any files, to ensure that your content is accepted and can be sold.

Research topic for your images

When researching topics for your stock photography files, there are a few key things to consider:

1.   *Popular trends*: One of the best ways to ensure that your files will be in demand is to keep an eye on popular trends in photography. Look at what subjects are currently popular in the stock photography market and consider creating files that align with those trends.

2.   *Target audience*: Another important factor to consider when researching topics for your stock photography images is your *target audience*. Think about the types of customers who might be interested in purchasing your files, and create content that aligns with their interests and needs.

3.   *Seasonal events*: Seasonal events, holidays and special occasions can be a great source of inspiration when researching topics for your stock photography files. Capture moments, emotions and the atmosphere of those events and create files that will be relevant to them.

4.   *Niche subjects*: Consider exploring niche subjects that are not as popular in the stock photography market. By focusing on a specific subject matter, you can create a unique portfolio that stands out from the competition.

5.   *Conduct a keyword research*: Before uploading your files, you can conduct a *keyword research* to identify the most search terms used by customers. Identify the keywords that are relevant to your images and make sure to use them when describing your files.

6.   *Analyze the competition*: Look at what other photographers are doing in your niche or on your topic. See what types of images are popular, but also look for *gaps in the market*.

7.   *Look for inspiration everywhere*: Inspiration for your stock photography files can come from anywhere, whether it's a walk through nature, a trip to the city, or just watching people go about their daily lives. Be open to new ideas and keep your camera with you at all times.

By following these tips you can create files that are in high demand and will appeal to a wide range of customers.

Stock websites for **designers**

Most stock photography websites also allow designers to upload and sell their own design elements, such as icons, patterns, mock-up and templates. This can be a great way for designers to earn money from their work and expand their portfolio.

Stock photography websites provide a great opportunity for designers to showcase their work, find new customers and earn money from their creations. They can also be a great source of inspiration, and a way to discover new trends and techniques in visual design.

Conclusion

Becoming a stock contributor offers an exciting opportunity to showcase your *creative work*, whether you're a photographer, designer, illustrator, or other visual artist. By joining stock photography websites, you can reach a global audience, monetize your talent, and contribute to a wide range of creative projects.

While the earning potential varies based on factors like the quality of your work, *market demand*, and your dedication to the craft, the possibility of generating a sustainable income is within reach. With persistence, ongoing learning, and adaptability to changing industry trends, you can navigate the competitive landscape and establish yourself as a *successful stock contributor*.

Remember that starting your journey as a stock contributor requires building a strong portfolio, *understanding the guidelines of each platform*, and optimizing your content for searchability. It's crucial to stay informed about market trends, identify niche opportunities, and continuously refine your skills to create captivating and relevant visual assets.

Networking within the stock photography community, leveraging social media, and promoting your work can help you expand your reach and attract potential buyers. Collaboration with other contributors and seeking feedback from the community can also contribute to your growth as an artist.

While the path to success may involve initial investments of time and money, the rewards of seeing your work appreciated, used, and earning income can be highly gratifying. By embracing the challenges and opportunities that arise along the way, you can develop your artistic vision, improve your technical skills, and achieve recognition in the dynamic world of stock photography.

If you have a passion for visual expression and a desire to share your creativity with the world, becoming a stock contributor can be a fulfilling and rewarding endeavor. Embrace the possibilities, let your imagination soar, and embark on the journey of turning your artistic talent into a thriving business.

#2

Amazon Associate

Amazon's Affiliate Advantage

Becoming an Amazon Associate is a great way to earn money by promoting products listed on Amazon.com. As an associate, you will be provided with unique links and banners that you can share on your website, social media, or anywhere else on the internet. When someone clicks on one of your links and makes a purchase on Amazon, you will *earn a commission* on the sale. The process of becoming an Amazon Associate is simple and straightforward. You will need to sign up for an account, agree to the terms and conditions, and then you can start earning money by promoting products.

Is Amazon Associate for you?

Becoming an Amazon Associate is ideal for anyone who has a platform to promote products, such as a website, blog, social media account, or an email list. It is also ideal for anyone who wants to earn money passively by promoting products they believe in. It can be especially beneficial for individuals or businesses in the e-commerce, retail, or online marketing space, as well as content creators, influencers, and bloggers who want to monetize their platforms. For those who want to get started with *affiliate marketing*, it's a great entry point as Amazon is a well-known and trusted brand with a wide variety of products.

Skillset

To become an Amazon Associate, you do not need any specific skills, but there are some things that can increase your chances of success:

1.   *Knowledge of online marketing*: Understanding how to drive traffic and generate sales through online channels can help you promote Amazon products effectively.

2.   *Good communication skills*: Being able to effectively communicate with your audience and persuade them to make a purchase is important.

3.   *Writing skills*: If you plan to promote products through a blog or website, you should have good writing skills to create engaging and informative content.

4.   *Understanding of SEO*: Knowing how to optimize your website or content for search engines can help you drive more traffic to your Amazon Associate links.

5.   *Knowledge of the products you want to promote*: If you want to promote specific products, you should have a good understanding of the products and their features.

Having these skills is not mandatory but they can help you to be more successful as an Amazon Associate.

Time

Getting started as an Amazon Associate is relatively quick and easy. The actual process of signing up for an account and getting approved can take as little as a few minutes. The time required to start seeing results will depend on the **effort and resources** you put into **promoting** the products.

Once you are approved as an Amazon Associate, you can start creating links and banners to promote products. It may take some time to drive traffic to your links and start generating sales.

If you're planning to promote products through your website or blog, it could take some additional time to create content and optimize it for search engines.

You can get started as an Amazon Associate in a matter of minutes, but it may take some time and effort to start generating income.

Choose the right product

Choosing the right products to promote as an Amazon Associate is crucial for your success. Here are a few tips on how to choose the right products:

1.   *Align with your niche or audience*: Choose products that align with your niche or that your audience is interested in. This will increase the chances of a purchase.

2.   *Look for **high-demand** and **high-profit** products*: Look for products that have high demand and a high-profit margin. These products will likely generate more sales and revenue for you.

3.   *Check the product reviews*: Look at the reviews of the product, check the star rating, and read some of the reviews to get an idea of the quality of the product.

4.   *Check the product's sales rank*: Check the product's sales rank on Amazon; products with higher sales rank tend to be more popular and can be more profitable to promote.

5.   *Look for **seasonal** products*: You can also consider promoting seasonal products, this way you can take advantage of the increased demand during specific periods of the year.

6.   *Try promoting products that you have personal experience with:* This will make it easier for you to write effective product reviews and make recommendations to potential buyers.

Take your time to you can choose the right products to promote as an Amazon Associate and increase your chances of success

How to integrate the links into your content?

There are several ways to integrate Amazon Associate links into your content, here are a few:

1.   *Text links*: You can include text links in your content, such as blog posts or articles, by *hyperlinking* specific keywords or phrases to the product on Amazon.

2.   *Image links*: You can also include image links in your content by embedding the Amazon link into an image of the product.

3.   *Call to Action*: You can also use a call to action in your content to encourage readers to click on your Amazon Associate link.

4.   *Product review*: You can write a product review and include your affiliate link within the article, this way, your audience could see your opinion about the product and decide if they want to purchase it or not.

5.   *Product comparison*: You can also include affiliate links by creating a product comparison, where you review and compare different products; this could help your audience to make a decision on which product to purchase.

6.   *Promotions, discounts, and deals*: you can use promotions, discounts, and deals to promote the products and include your affiliate link; this could encourage your audience to make a purchase.

When integrating links, you should **always disclose** that you are an Amazon Associate and that you may receive a commission for any purchases made through your links.

It's important to use the links in a natural way, don't overdo it, and don't make it look like you're just trying to sell something to your audience.

Can you use the images from Amazon?

As an Amazon Associate, you are allowed to use product images provided by Amazon to promote the products you are affiliated with. According to Amazon's Operating Agreement, you are permitted to use the product images, product descriptions, and customer reviews provided by Amazon on the Amazon website to promote products.

You should always use the images in accordance with Amazon's guidelines and terms of service and only use them to promote the products you are affiliated with.

Amazon also provides a feature called "Site Stripe" that allows you to quickly and easily generate image links and HTML code to use on your website or blog. This feature will automatically include your affiliate tracking code in the links, so you don't have to manually add it.

It's always a good idea to double-check the terms and conditions and guidelines of Amazon, as they may change over time.

You should also be aware of copyright laws, you should only use images that you have the right to use or that are in the public domain.

Generating traffic

Generating traffic is important for Amazon Associates because it directly affects your ability to make sales and earn commissions.

The more traffic you can drive to your Amazon Associate links, the more potential customers you have to make purchases through those links. This means that the more traffic you can generate, the more potential revenue you can earn as an Amazon Associate.

Driving traffic to your Amazon Associate links also helps to increase your visibility and credibility as an affiliate marketer.

The more people who visit your website or social media pages and click on your links, the more likely you are to be seen as trustworthy and credible.

Generating traffic also helps you to create a sense of urgency and scarcity around the products you are promoting. This can encourage more people to make purchases through your links.

All in all, generating traffic is important for Amazon Associates because it helps to increase the number of potential customers, which in turn increases the potential revenue earned through commissions.

Build trust

Building trust with your website visitors is an important aspect of being an Amazon Associate. Here are some ideas on how you can build trust with your customers:

1.   *Be transparent*: Clearly disclose that you are an Amazon Associate and that you may receive a commission for any purchases made through your links. This helps to build trust by being open and honest about your relationship with Amazon.

2.   *Provide valuable and honest information*: Offer valuable and honest information about the products you are promoting. This will help to build trust by providing your audience with accurate and reliable information.

3.   *Use social proof*: Share customer reviews and testimonials of the products you are promoting. This will help to *build trust* by

showing that other customers have had positive experiences with the products.

4.   *Be responsive*: Respond to comments, questions, and feedback from your audience. This will help to build trust by showing that you are *engaged and interested* in your audience's needs and concerns.

5.   *Build a community*: Encourage engagement by building a community of like-minded individuals who share an interest in the products and services you are promoting.

6.   *Show your expertise*: Share your personal experience, knowledge, and expertise about the products you're promoting. This will help to build trust by showing that you have a *personal investment* in the products and that you have done your research.

Building trust with your website visitors can increase the chances of them making a purchase through your Amazon Associate links.

How to make money with the Amazon Associate program?

There are several ways to make money as an Amazon Associate, here are a few:

1.   *Promote products through your website or blog*: By including Amazon Associate links in your content, you can earn a commission on any sales made through those links.

2.   *Use social media*: Share your Amazon Associate links on social media platforms such as Facebook, Twitter, and Instagram to drive traffic to your links and earn commissions on sales.

3.   *Email marketing*: Include Amazon Associate links in your email campaigns to promote products and earn commissions.

4.   *Influencer marketing*: If you have a large following on social media platforms, you can work with brands to promote their products and earn commissions on sales made through your links.

5.   *Create a niche website*: Build a website focused on a specific niche such as outdoor gear, kitchen appliances, etc. And promote related products through Amazon Associate program.

6.   *Use affiliate marketing*: Use affiliate marketing to promote Amazon products, this could be done by creating product reviews, product comparisons, and more.

The amount of money you can make as an Amazon Associate will depend on the amount of traffic you can drive to your links and the number of sales you can generate. The more traffic and sales you can generate, the more money you make.

Which Amazon Associate program to sign up for? Can you use links from different countries?

It does matter for which Amazon Associate program you sign up. *Each Amazon country has its own program*, and you will need to **sign up separately** for each one if you want to promote products from multiple countries.

Each program has its own terms and conditions, commission rates, and available products, so you have to research and compare the different programs to determine which one is best for you.

Once you are an Amazon Associate for a specific country, you can use links from that country to promote products to customers within that country. You will not be able to use links from one country to promote products to customers in another country unless you are an associate of that country too.

Some countries may have restrictions on which products can be promoted or shipped to that country, so you should also check the availability of products before signing up for a specific program.

You should also be aware that the commission rate and the payment method may vary depending on the country, so you should check this as well.

Conclusion

Becoming an Amazon Associate opens up a world of opportunities for individuals and businesses alike. With the potential to earn **passive income** by promoting products from the world's largest e-commerce platform, the Amazon Associate program offers a pathway to monetizing your online presence and leveraging your influence.

As an Amazon Associate, you have the flexibility to choose from millions of products to promote, catering to various niches and industries. Whether you have a website, blog, social media following, or email list, you can seamlessly integrate Amazon Associate links and banners into your content, providing value to your audience while earning a commission on qualifying purchases.

While the journey as an Amazon Associate may vary for each person, success often comes down to strategic promotion, targeted marketing efforts, and fostering trust with your audience. By selecting the right products, generating traffic, and building a rapport with your visitors, you can increase your chances of converting clicks into sales.

As with any entrepreneurial pursuit, patience and perseverance is the key. It takes time to establish your online presence, build an engaged audience, and optimize your promotional strategies.

Becoming an Amazon Associate is more than just a way to earn income; it's an opportunity to connect people with products they desire, facilitate informed purchasing decisions, and play a role in the vast ecosystem of online commerce.

Whether you're a content creator, influencer, blogger, or entrepreneur, consider embarking on the path of becoming an Amazon Associate. Embrace the possibilities and build a thriving online business while partnering with one of the world's most trusted brands.

#3

Make Money With AI Art

A Cash Canvas

Artificial intelligence (AI) art refers to the use of AI technology to create or assist in the creation of artwork. This can include using machine learning algorithms to generate images or videos, using AI to assist in the creation of digital art. The earning potential for AI art can vary depending on the specific application and the demand for the resulting artwork. Some artists are developing AI-based businesses and services, such as creating custom AI art for clients. As the field of AI art continues to evolve, the earning potential for AI artists will likely increase as well.

Skillset

The fun part of AI is that you can have skills but you actually don't need them. You need only imagination of what you want to create and the AI will create it for you. This applies to images, music, animation, and even videos. You will still need to have some descriptive skills to "tell" the AI what you want, but there are books to help you with that and even tools that you can use. But for that later on. You can browse my book **"Midjourney Digest: MAKE AI ART THAT SELLS"** available on Amazon's Kindle Unlimited to help you create interesting and innovative prompts. The book is an extensive list of words, that you can add to your prompts to bring your art to the next level.

Book preview

"Midjourney Digest: MAKE AI ART THAT SELLS":

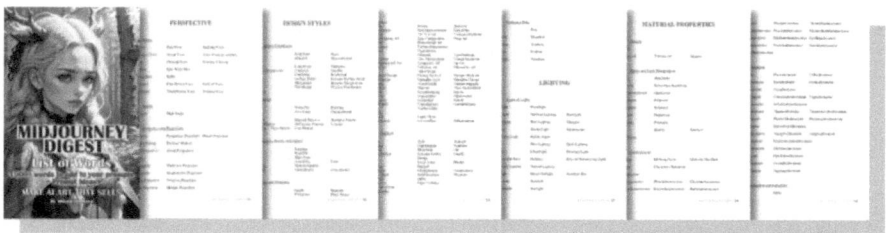

Where to sell your AI Art?

There are a number of places where AI art can be sold, including:

1.   *Online marketplaces*: Websites such as ArtStaion specialize in selling digital art, and have sections dedicated to AI art. These marketplaces provide a platform for artists to showcase and sell their AI art to a wider audience.

2.   *Crowdfunding platforms*: Crowdfunding platforms like Kickstarter and Indiegogo can also be used to raise funds to create and sell AI art. This approach allows artists to get financial support from a community of people who are interested in their work and want to see it come to fruition. It also allows them to reach a wider audience.

3.   *Personal Website (Portfolio)*: Artists can also sell their AI artworks through their personal websites, such as Behance, Dribbble, or their personal portfolio sites. This allows artists to have full control over their online presence and reach an audience directly. Artists can also sell their works through their own e-

commerce system, which can save them from paying commission to third parties.

4.   *NFT Marketplaces*: Non-fungible token (NFT) marketplaces like OpenSea and Rarible allow artists to sell digital art as unique, verifiable, and collectible assets.

5.   *Social Media*: Use social media platforms like Instagram, Twitter, and TikTok to showcase and sell your digital art to a wider audience.

6.   *Digital Downloads*: Sell digital copies of your artwork as high-resolution downloads on your website or on online marketplaces such as Etsy or Gumroad.

7.   *Stock Websites*: You can also sell your AI art on stock websites like Adobe Stock.

8.   *Freelance Art Services*: Offer your AI art services to clients who need customized artwork for their websites, social media, or marketing campaigns.

The above options are not mutually exclusive and an artist can use multiple ways to showcase and sell their AI art.

Artstation

ArtStation is a popular online platform that cater to the digital art and entertainment industries. The platform serves as community where artists, designers, and creative professionals can showcase their artwork, connect with other artists, and find opportunities in the industry.

ArtStation (www.artstation.com) is a leading platform that focuses on various forms of digital art, including concept art, illustration, 3D modeling, and animation. It offers artists the ability to create professional portfolios, showcase their artwork, and even sell prints, digital downloads, and other products through the ArtStation Marketplace. Artists can also participate in challenges, access job listings, and connect with potential clients or employers.

To sell art on ArtStation, artists can set up a store on the ArtStation Marketplace and upload their artworks for sale. ArtStation takes a commission on each sale made through the platform.

ArtStation is a reputable platform with a large user base and is well-regarded in the art and entertainment industries. Success on this platform relies on the quality of the artwork, marketing efforts, and engagement with the community.

Gumroad

Gumroad (https://gumroad.com/) is a platform that revolutionizes the way artists, including AI creators, share and sell their imaginative works. With its user-friendly setup and global reach, Gumroad provides a seamless avenue for artists to showcase their masterpieces to a diverse audience. There is an interesting option when you set your price per product, you can choose that people can pay how much they think they should pay. This way you can give more freedom to your customers and potentially make more sales.

Image generation tools

There are a number of platforms and tools that can be used to create AI art, including:

1.   **Midjourney**   (https://www.midjourney.com/): Midjourney is an innovative AI-based platform that empowers artists to create stunning and unique artworks using advanced machine learning algorithms. With its user-friendly interface and customizable parameters, Midjourney offers a seamless experience for artists exploring the world of AI-generated art.

2. **Stable Diffusion** (https://www.stablediffusion.com/): Stable Diffusion utilizes cutting-edge AI techniques to generate beautiful and stable visual art pieces. This platform offers artists an array of tools to experiment with various styles and parameters, enabling them to create mesmerizing AI-generated artwork.

3. **StarryAI** (https://www.starryai.com/): StarryAI is an AI art generator that specializes in creating breathtaking scenes inspired by famous artists such as Vincent van Gogh. Artists can use StarryAI to produce mesmerizing and dreamlike artworks with ease.

4. **DALL-E 2** (https://openai.com/dall-e-2/): Developed by OpenAI, DALL-E 2 is a state-of-the-art language model that generates creative and surreal images based on textual prompts. With DALL-E 2, artists can explore a wide range of ideas and concepts to inspire their AI-generated art.

The last version was out in Oct. 2023 is **DALL-E 3** which has significant improvements over DALL-E 2.

5. **Nightcafe** (https://www.nightcafe.studio/): Nightcafe combines the power of AI and human creativity to produce stunning AI-generated portraits and landscapes. With its AI-assisted painting tools, artists can delve into new dimensions of artistic expression.

6. **Dream by Wombo** (https://dream.ai/create): Dream by Wombo is an AI art generator that brings your wildest imaginations to life. Artists can create imaginative and whimsical artworks using Dream by Wombo's advanced AI technology.

7. **BigSleep** (https://github.com/lucidrains/big-sleep): BigSleep is an open-source AI art generator that utilizes powerful models to create mesmerizing and intricate artworks. It offers artists flexibility in tweaking parameters to achieve desired visual effects.

8. **Deep Dream Generator**
(https://deepdreamgenerator.com/): Deep Dream Generator is a user-friendly AI art platform that transforms text into trippy and surreal artworks using deep learning algorithms.

9. **Wonder** (https://www.wonder-ai.com/): Wonder is an AI art generator that transforms your selfies into imaginative and dreamlike portraits. It offers users an easy way to explore creative possibilities with their images. You have to pay for this service.

10. **Artbreeder** (https://www.artbreeder.com/): Artbreeder is a popular AI art platform that allows artists to blend, combine, and evolve images using advanced AI techniques. Artists can create unique and inspiring AI-generated artworks with ease.

11. **Stablecog** (https://www.stablecog.com/): Stablecog utilizes AI technology to generate mesmerizing and stable images

that captivate the imagination. It offers a seamless and user-friendly experience for artists exploring the possibilities of AI art.

12. **Runway ML** (https://runwayml.com/): Runway ML is an AI art platform that empowers artists with pre-trained models and creative tools to produce captivating AI-generated art. It offers a wide range of artistic possibilities for experimentation and exploration.

13. **Deep AI** (https://deepai.org/): Deep AI is an AI platform that offers various AI-powered tools, including AI art generation. Artists can leverage AI algorithms to create mesmerizing and imaginative artworks, pushing the boundaries of their creative expression. Deep AI provides a simple and user-friendly interface, making it accessible to artists of all levels to experiment with AI-generated art.

14. **Adobe Express** (https://www.adobe.com/express/): Adobe Express is a free software created by Adobe, offering a wide array of AI tools like removing of backgrounds, text to image, text effects and many more. It's definetelly something to try out.

15. **Ideogram** (https://ideogram.ai/): Ideaogram is the coolest and most popular AI image generator at the moment. First, because it is free and second, it can also generate text! Wow, yes! First of it's kind. Say, for example, you want a card that says "Happy Birthday Anne!", it would create a stunning design using even the proper punctuation ☺ Its users generate 3.5 million images weekly so hurry up and use the opportunity while it's still free.

16. I am going to add to this list Fotor (https://www.fotor.com/): While not exclusively an AI art generator, Fotor offers a range of AI-powered tools and filters that artists can use to enhance and transform their photos into stunning works of art.

Please note that some platforms might be continuously evolving or have limited access, and it is always essential to verify their current status and offerings.

The cost of using these platforms can vary, some are free to use, while others have a free version and a paid version with more features. It's a good idea to research the specific platform's pricing and features before using it.

The rights over the art created can vary depending on the terms of service of the platform, the type of algorithm used, and the laws of the country where the artist is located. In general, the artist retains the rights to the artworks created, but it's important to read the terms of service of the platform and consult with a lawyer if necessary to fully understand the rights and responsibilities related to the artworks created.

Stock photo websites and AI Art

As AI-generated art is a relatively new form of digital art, not all stock photo websites accept them as a category of content. Some stock photo websites have started to accept AI-generated artworks. The acceptance of AI-generated artworks and the specific guidelines and requirements may vary among stock photo websites. Here are a few examples of stock photo websites that accept AI-generated art:

•   Adobe Stock: https://stock.adobe.com/ is a stock photo website that accepts AI-generated artworks. They have a broad category for digital art, and AI-generated artworks may be included in that category.

•   Dreamstime: https://www.dreamstime.com/ is a stock photo platform that accepts AI-generated images. Important is to read their guidelines and requirements as they differ from the guidelines of Adobe Stock.

•   Freepik: https://www.freepik.com/ is an online platform that offers a vast collection of high-quality graphic resources for personal and commercial use. From vector graphics and illustrations to photos and templates. They also accept AI-generated images.

These are a few examples and it's best to check the terms of service and submission guidelines of the stock photo website before submitting AI-generated artworks, as the acceptance and specific guidelines may vary among different websites.

Keep in mind that AI-generated artworks may be subject to copyright laws, and the artist should ensure that they have the rights to the artwork before submitting it to a stock photo website. Do NOT use the names of other artists when creating images for stock websites. This can lead to a lawsuit as you don't have the legal right to sell this type of works. Try to be unique and creative and create your own style.

Important: Alamy, iStock, and Shutterstock are NOT accepting AI-generated images.

Popular themes (for stock images)

Here are some popular topics that are good to concentrate on when creating stock imagery. Always think: "What do people need?" I recommend using ChatGPT to create a list of keywords regarding each topic you create. Then build your prompts around these keywords to have better reach and accessibility.

1. *Business and finance*: themes such as office spaces, business meetings, financial charts, and diagrams.

2. *Technology and innovation*: themes such as smartphones, laptops, internet, and other digital devices, as well as concepts like IoT, blockchain, and AI.

3. *Nature and landscape*: themes such as mountains, beaches, forests, sunsets, and other natural environments.

4. *People and lifestyle*: themes such as families, friends, couples, and diverse groups of people engaging in different activities, such as traveling, working, or relaxing.

5. *Urban and city*: themes such as cityscapes, skylines, public transportation, and city life.

6. *Health and wellness*: themes such as yoga, meditation, healthy food, and fitness.

7. *Food and drink*: themes such as cooking, dining, and different types of cuisine.

8. *Travel and tourism*: themes such as landmarks, popular tourist destinations, and different cultures.

9.	*Education and learning*: themes such as classrooms, textbooks, lectures, and students of all ages.

10.	*Creative and artistic*: themes such as design, art, music, and photography.

11.	*Industry and infrastructure*: themes such as factories, construction sites, and transportation.

12.	*Social issues and politics*: themes such as climate change, inequality, and social justice.

13.	*Fashion and beauty*: themes such as clothing, hairstyles, makeup, and accessories.

14.	*Holiday and special events*: themes such as Christmas, Valentine's Day, and other holidays or special events.

15.	*Science and research*: themes such as laboratory, experiments, and scientific breakthroughs.

Other ways to sell your images

How you can leverage the power of social media and crowdfunding to showcase and monetize your AI-generated art. We'll focus on two major platforms: Instagram and Patreon, where you can gain a loyal fanbase and turn your passion for AI art into a sustainable source of income.

Step 1: Create an Instagram Account for Your AI Art

Start by setting up an Instagram account dedicated to showcasing your AI-generated masterpieces. Choose an engaging username that reflects your *artistic style and brand.* Write a compelling bio that introduces yourself and highlights your passion for AI art.

Step 2: Post Regularly to Engage Your Audience

Consistency is key to building a devoted following on Instagram. Regularly post your AI art with thoughtful captions that give insights into your creative process or the inspiration behind your creations. *Engage with your audience* by responding to comments and using relevant hashtags to reach a broader audience.

Step 3: Create a Patreon Account

Patreon (https://www.patreon.com/) is a popular crowdfunding platform that enables creators to receive ongoing financial support from their fans. Create a Patreon account and set up tiers offering exclusive perks to your patrons, such as early access to artwork, behind-the-scenes content, or personalized AI-generated art.

Step 4: Link Patreon to Your Instagram Profile

Maximize visibility by adding your Patreon link to your Instagram profile. Encourage your followers to support your art by becoming patrons and gain access to exclusive rewards. Regularly remind your audience about your Patreon page through Instagram posts and stories.

Step 5: Offer Exclusive Content to Patrons

To entice potential patrons, provide *exclusive content* and benefits for each tier. This could include monthly digital downloads of your AI art, live Q&A sessions, or even personalized

AI-generated artwork for higher-tier patrons. The more value you offer, the more likely patrons will support you. Tiers are only an option, you can also have one tier for all, whatever suits you.

Step 6: Engage and Nurture Your Patreon Community

Create a welcoming and interactive space for your patrons. Engage with them through personalized messages, polls, and community updates. Listen to their feedback and consider their input in your future AI art projects.

Bonus: Repeat the same process on Pixiv

For a broader reach, consider sharing your AI art on Pixiv (https://www.pixiv.net/en/), a popular art community in Japan and beyond. Pixiv allows you to gain exposure to a global audience of art enthusiasts, connecting with a diverse community of like-minded creatives.

You can repeat the process on as many platforms as you want to help you find more fans and supporters.

Combining the power of Instagram and Patreon offers a unique opportunity for AI artists to showcase their creations, build a loyal fanbase, and gain financial support from patrons who believe in their talent. By nurturing your online presence and offering exclusive perks to your supporters, you can turn your passion for AI art into a thriving artistic journey. Remember, dedication and engagement are the keys to success in building your AI art empire.

Sell your prompts

You can also monetize your creative ideas by simply selling your prompts. PromptBase (www.promptbase.com) is a revolutionary platform, that welcomes creators to sell their prompts specifically designed for AI art generation. Whether you're an artist, writer, or simply brimming with imaginative ideas, PromptBase provides a space to share and profit from your creativity.

There is a small catch, for now, PromptBase accepts prompts only for the following platforms: DALL·E, Midjourney, Stable Diffusion, and ChatGPT. They might expand their submissions in the future. By offering prompts tailored to these cutting-edge technologies, you empower AI artists to produce captivating and innovative artwork based on your creative inspiration and you get paid for it.

Use AI to find out keywords from an image

Check out this pretty cool tool that you can use to find out keywords from an already existing image called Pixify (https://pixify.io/ai-keywording-tool).

For example, you like the image on the right. The steps are: you upload the image into the tool (website), and then it generates a title, description, and keywords. Here are the ones that it generated for this picture:

Title: Adorable Cartoon Dog Character - Cute and Friendly Pet Companion

Description: Adorable animated dog showcases friendship and connection between humans and pets.

Keywords: animal, animal themes, canine, cartoon, dog, domestic animals, mammal, one animal, pet, adorable, animated, breed, cartoonish, character, companion, cute, doggy, domestic, friendship, furry

Pretty cool, right?

How to use this tool to your advantage?

1. Use it when you upload your images to sites like Adobe Stock, use the *title*, *description*, and *keywords*, add your own keywords, change it how you want, and make it unique and interesting. Have in mind that when you upload images to Adobe Stock, they are not very happy if the names of the files are image01.jpg, image02.jpg, etc. The images most probably will get rejected. Use this tool to create *unique titles with one click*.

Workflow: **Generate an image > upload to pixify.io > copy keywords/title/description > submit to Adobe Stock**

2. Another way how you can use it is to create your own prompts with the idea to sell them afterward. Determine the keywords from the desired picture, to be safe use *public domain pictures*. We are taking again the picture with the dog as an example. Copy the title, description, and keywords into chatGPT and ask it to create a prompt based on the following information.

After it creates the prompt, edit it to your liking, and test it in the platform that is intended for, for example, Midjourney. Alter the prompt until you are happy with the result.

Now you have a great prompt to sell on PromptBase, using only AI tools and a bit of imagination.

Workflow: **Upload an image to pixify.io > generate keywords, title, description > add the information into chatGPT > generate prompt > test it in the intended platform > sell the prompt on Promptbase**

After using the keywording tool for a while it will ask you to register with your email. You can do that and continue to use it for free.

Conclusion

Creating and selling AI art in its various forms offers a world of possibilities and opportunities for artists and art enthusiasts. With the advancements in artificial intelligence and machine learning, artists can explore new frontiers of creativity, pushing the boundaries of traditional art forms.

AI-generated art allows artists to tap into the potential of algorithms and data-driven processes, enabling the creation of unique and captivating artworks that may not have been possible through conventional methods. Whether it's AI-generated paintings, digital illustrations, music compositions, or even immersive experiences, the realm of AI art offers a wide range of expressive avenues.

The market for AI art continues to expand, with increasing interest from collectors, enthusiasts, and industry professionals. Artists have the opportunity to reach global audiences through online platforms and marketplaces dedicated to AI art. The potential for commercial success, recognition, and collaborations with innovative brands and institutions has never been greater.

While AI plays a significant role in the creation process, it is essential to remember that human creativity, imagination, and skill remain at the core of AI art. Artists have the power to infuse their unique vision, resulting in truly original and thought-provoking creations.

As the field of AI art evolves, it is crucial for artists to stay curious and adapt to emerging technologies. Exploring the intersection of art and technology not only offers personal growth and artistic fulfillment but also contributes to the broader conversation on the evolving role of AI in society.

Embrace the possibilities, experiment fearlessly, and let the fusion of art and AI inspire new forms of artistic expression. The world awaits the captivating and transformative creations that lie at the intersection of human imagination and artificial intelligence.

#4

Dropshipping

Your Online Store

Dropshipping is a business model where a retailer does not keep goods in stock, but instead transfers customer orders and shipment details to the manufacturer, another retailer, or a wholesaler. After your client makes the order they ship it straight to the customer. This allows the retailer to sell a *wide range of products* without having to invest in inventory or handle shipping and fulfillment. As a result, retailers can operate with lower overhead costs and can focus on marketing and customer acquisition.

Is dropshipping for you?

Dropshipping can be a good option for:

1.   Entrepreneurs or small business owners who want to start an e-commerce business with a low initial investment and minimal overhead costs.

2.   Online retailers who want to expand their product offerings without having to invest in additional inventory.

3.   Individuals who want to test the market for a new product before committing to purchasing large quantities.

4.   E-commerce store owners who want to try out multiple products before committing to a specific one.

5.   People who want to start an online business with a flexible schedule.

6.   Individuals who are looking to start an online business but have less experience in product sourcing and logistics.

Dropshipping also have some drawbacks such as higher price point and lack of control over the inventory, shipping and customer service. It's important to weigh the pros and cons before starting a dropshipping business.

Skillset

To start a successful dropshipping business, you will need a combination of the following skills:

1.   *Marketing*: Understanding how to attract and retain customers through various online marketing channels such as social media, search engine optimization (SEO), and paid advertising.

2.   *E-commerce*: Knowledge of how to set up and manage an online store, including website design, product listing, and checkout processes.

3.   *Product sourcing*: The ability to research and find reliable suppliers and manufacturers who can provide high-quality products at competitive prices.

4.   *Sales*: Having the ability to close deals and negotiate with suppliers and manufacturers.

5.   *Customer service*: Providing excellent customer service to build trust and loyalty with customers.

6.   *Data analysis*: Being able to analyze data to make informed business decisions, such as which products to stock or which marketing campaigns are most effective.

7.   *Adaptability:* Being able to adapt to changes in the market or customer preferences.

8.   *Technical skills*: Familiarity with e-commerce platforms and tools such as Shopify, Oberlo, Aliexpress, etc.

In addition to these skills, it's good to have a strong work ethic, good time management, and the ability to problem-solve.

Dropshipping sites

There are a large number of e-commerce platforms, such as Shopify, BigCommerce, WooCommerce for WordPress, etc, which are popular among dropshippers, as they offer various tools and apps to make it easy to set up and manage an online store, and to integrate with suppliers and manufacturers. There are many dropshipping suppliers and wholesalers available, such as AliExpress, Oberlo, and SaleHoo that allow retailers to easily find and source products to sell on their online stores. It's safe to say that there are a lot of dropshipping sites available, and the number is growing as e-commerce continues to evolve and expand.

The market

The e-commerce market is growing rapidly, and the dropshipping model is becoming more popular among entrepreneurs and small business owners. It is not necessarily oversaturated as there is always room for new players in the market, especially for those who can offer unique products or different value proposition.

The market for certain products may be oversaturated. Conducting a market research before starting a dropshipping business to identify potential competition can help you see if there is a demand for the products you plan to sell. If the market is already saturated, it may be more difficult to gain a foothold and stand out among competitors.

As more people are starting dropshipping businesses, competition for customers is also increasing, and it's becoming more difficult to attract customers and make sales.

The market for dropshipping is still growing and offers opportunities, and if you did proper research before starting a business you should be prepared for the competition.

Chance of success

The chance of success in any business venture, including a dropshipping business, depends on many factors such as the market conditions, the competition, your business model and strategy, your skills and experience, and your ability to adapt to changes.

There are many successful dropshipping businesses, but there are also many that fail. A key factor in the success of a dropshipping business is the ability to find a niche market, offer unique products, and build a strong brand. Having a solid marketing strategy, providing excellent customer service, and continuously improving your business based on data and customer feedback can also increase your chances of success.

Starting a dropshipping business or any other business requires hard work, dedication, and the willingness to learn and adapt. It's not a get-rich-quick scheme, and you should be realistic about the time and effort required to build a successful business.

With the right approach, a *solid business plan*, and a bit of luck, the chances of success can be increased.

Tools

There are many tools available to help with marketing a dropshipping business, including:

1.   *Google Analytics*: Helps track website traffic and analyze customer behavior, allowing you to optimize your marketing strategy and improve the customer experience.

2.   *Social media marketing tools*: Hootsuite, Later, Buffer, Sprout Social, etc, can help you schedule and automate social media posts, track engagement, and analyze your social media performance.

3.   *Email marketing tools*: MailChimp, Constant Contact, and Campaign Monitor, etc, allow you to create and send email

campaigns, segment your email list, and track the performance of your emails.

4. *SEO tools*: Ahrefs, SEMrush, and Moz, etc, help you optimize your website and content for search engines, track your rankings, and analyze your competition.

5. *Advertising tools*: Google Ads, Facebook Ads, and Instagram Ads, etc, allow you to create and manage paid advertising campaigns, target specific audiences, and track the performance of your ads.

6. *Retargeting tools*: Adroll, Perfect Audience, and Retargeting.biz, etc, allow you to target ads to people who have visited your website but haven't made a purchase yet.

7. *Product research tools*: Jungle Scout, Helium 10, and Viral Launch, etc, help you research and identify profitable products to sell and spy on your competitors.

8. *Live chat and customer service*: Tawk.to, Drift, and LiveChat, etc, allow you to provide real-time customer support and help build trust and loyalty with customers.

E-commerce tools

There are many tools available to help with e-commerce and managing a dropshipping business, including:

1. *E-commerce platforms*: Shopify, BigCommerce, WooCommerce for WordPress, etc, provide an all-in-one solution for setting up and managing an online store, including website design, product listing, checkout, and payment processing.

2.   *Order and inventory management*: TradeGecko, Ordoro, and Skubana, etc, help you manage orders, inventory, and fulfillments from multiple sales channels in one place.

3.   *Product and supplier management*: Oberlo, AliExpress, and SaleHoo, etc, help you find and source products from suppliers and manufacturers, and manage your inventory.

4.   *Payment gateway*: PayPal, Stripe, and Square, etc, allow you to securely process payments from customers on your website.

5.   *Analytics and reporting*: Google Analytics, Omniconvert, and Mixpanel, etc, provide insights into your website traffic, customer behavior, and sales performance, allowing you to make data-driven decisions.

6.   *Marketing and automation*: Klaviyo, Autopilot Journeys, Omnisend, Rejoiner, and Drip, etc, help you automate email marketing and customer communication.

7.   *Accounting and bookkeeping*: QuickBooks, Xero, and Wave, etc, help you manage your finances, create invoices, and track expenses.

Tools for product analysis, spotting the trends, researching manufacturers

There are many tools available to help with product analysis and research, including:

1.   *Product research tools*: Jungle Scout, Helium 10, and Viral Launch, etc. help you research and identify profitable products to

sell, by showing you data such as best-selling products, estimated sales, and competition analysis.

2.   *Keyword research tools*: Google Keyword Planner, Ahrefs, and SEMrush, etc. allow you to research and identify profitable keywords for your products and optimize your product listings for search engines.

3.   *Product tracking tools*: Keepa and CamelCamelCamel, help you track the price history and sales rank of products on different e-commerce platforms.

4.   *Trend analysis tools*: Google Trends, Trend Hunter, and SEMrush, etc. allow you to research and identify popular products and trends in your niche market.

5.   *Product sourcing sites*: Alibaba, Global Sources, and ThomasNet, etc. help you find and research manufacturers, wholesalers, and suppliers for your products.

6.   *Product review analysis tools*: ReviewMeta, Fakespot, and Review Analytics, etc. help you analyze customer reviews and feedback of products, giving you an insight into which products are well-received by customers and which ones are not.

Data analysis tools

There are many tools available to help with data analysis, including:

1.   *Data visualization tools*: Tableau, Power BI, and Looker Studio, etc. help you visualize and present data in an easy-to-understand format, such as charts, graphs, and dashboards.

2.   *Business intelligence tools*: Domo, SAP Business Objects, and IBM Cognos Analytics, etc. provide a comprehensive set of data analysis and reporting features, such as data warehousing, reporting, and dashboards.

3.   *Data mining tools*: RapidMiner, KNIME, and Orange Data Mining, etc. allow you to extract patterns and insights from large data sets, and can be used for predictive modeling and machine learning.

4.   *Excel add-ins*: Power Query, Power Pivot, and Solver, etc. provide advanced data analysis and modeling capabilities within the Microsoft Excel environment.

5.   *SQL*: SQL (Structured Query Language) is a programming language used for managing and manipulating data in relational databases. It allows you to extract, modify, and analyze data in a structured way

6.   *Python and R*: Python and R are programming languages that provide powerful data analysis and visualization libraries, such as Pandas, NumPy, and Matplotlib for Python and ggplot2, dplyr, and tidyr for R.

There are many other tools available, and it's important to find the ones that work best for your business. Also, keep in mind that these tools are just a small part of a larger data analysis strategy. A good *data analysis strategy* should be based on a deep understanding of your business objectives and the data that's important to achieving them.

Cost to set up a dropshipping website

Setting up a dropshipping website involves several steps and can vary in cost depending on the specific platform and tools you choose to use. Here's a general overview of the process:

1.   *Choose an e-commerce platform*: Shopify, BigCommerce, and WooCommerce for WordPress or other. They offer various tools and apps to make it easy to set up and manage an online store, and to integrate with suppliers and manufacturers.

2.   *Choose a domain name*: You can purchase a domain name from a registrar such as GoDaddy, Namecheap, etc. This is typically an annual cost.

3.   *Choose a hosting provider*: Many e-commerce platforms include hosting, but if you want to host your website with other providers, you can choose from Bluehost, HostGator, etc. This is typically a monthly or annual cost.

4.   *Set up your online store*: Customize your website's design, layout, and functionality, add products, and set up payment and shipping options.

5.   *Find and source products*: Use product sourcing tools like Oberlo, AliExpress, and SaleHoo to find and source products from suppliers and manufacturers.

6.   *Set up marketing and advertising*: Use tools such as Google Ads, Facebook Ads, and email marketing to attract customers to your store.

The cost of setting up a dropshipping website can vary depending on the specific platform and tools you choose to use, but generally, it can cost anywhere from a few hundred dollars to a couple of thousands of dollars, depending on the features you need and the level of customization you require.

For example, if you use Shopify as your e-commerce platform, the basic plan starts at $29/month, and you would need to pay for the cost of a domain name and hosting (around $15/year) and any additional apps or plugins you might need. If you use Oberlo, which is a popular app for product sourcing and order fulfillment, the basic plan starts at $29.90/month.

Keep in mind that these costs are ongoing expenses and you will also need to factor in costs for marketing and advertising, customer service, and other business expenses.

General business models: How to choose the right business model?

There are several business models that can be used for a dropshipping business, including:

1.   *Niche dropshipping*: Focusing on a specific niche market, such as a particular product category or customer demographic, and sourcing products from suppliers that cater to that market.

2.   *General store*: Carrying a wide variety of products from different suppliers and categories in order to appeal to a broad customer base.

3.   *Branding and Private Label*: Developing your own brand and creating your own products, often through working with a manufacturer to create a unique product or by branding a pre-existing product.

4.   *Subscription-based*: A business model where customers pay a recurring fee for a product or service, such as a monthly box of products or access to a membership site.

5.   *Physical product arbitrage*: A business model where a retailer purchases products from one market and resells them in another market, often taking advantage of price differences.

6.   *Print on Demand*: A business model where a retailer creates a product design and sends it to a supplier who will only print and ship the product when an order is placed. Find out more about print on demand in Chapter #8 POD Sites: *Prints and Profits,* page 123.

These business models are not mutually exclusive, and a dropshipping business can also combine elements from different models to create a unique approach. Choosing the right business model will depend on your personal strengths, the market demand, and the level of competition. Consider the costs and resources required to start and operate the business model, as well as the potential for scalability and profitability.

Choose the right business model for your dropshipping business

Choosing the right business model for your dropshipping business depends on a variety of factors, including your personal strengths, the *market demand,* and the level of competition. Here are a few steps you can take to help you choose the right business model for your dropshipping business:

1.   *Research the market*: Look at the trends, the competition, and the customer demographics in your niche. Identify what

products are in demand, what types of customers are buying them, and what the competition looks like.

2.   *Identify your strengths and weaknesses*: Consider your own strengths and weaknesses, such as your skills, experience, and resources, and how they align with the different business models.

3.   *Consider the costs and resources*: Each business model has different costs and resources required, such as sourcing products, creating a brand, and marketing. Make sure you understand these costs and resources and that you have the means to support them.

4.   *Analyze the scalability and profitability*: Consider how each business model can scale and what the potential for profitability is.

5.   *Test and experiment*: Once you've narrowed down your options, start testing and experimenting with different models to see what works best for you.

6.   *Seek advice*: Don't hesitate to reach out to professionals, such as business consultants or coaches, who can provide guidance and support to help you make the right choice.

Choosing the right business model for your dropshipping business is an important step in ensuring success. It's essential to conduct thorough research on the market, identify your strengths and weaknesses, and consider the costs and resources required for each business model. It may be helpful to test and experiment with different models before making a final decision, and consider seeking advice from professionals. Remember, the key to success is to choose a business model that aligns with your strengths, the market demand, and your resources, and that has the *potential for scalability and profitability*.

Build a business plan

Building a business plan for a dropshipping business is a key step in ensuring the success of your venture. A business plan is a document that outlines your business goals, strategies, and actions to achieve them. Here are a few steps to help you build a business plan for your dropshipping business:

1. *Define your business goals*: Clearly define your business goals, such as increasing sales, reaching a certain number of customers, or reaching a certain level of profitability.

2. *Conduct market research*: Understand the market, your target customer, and your competition. Identify trends, customer needs, and potential suppliers and manufacturers.

3. *Develop your product and pricing strategy*: Identify the products you will sell, how you will source them, and how you will price them.

4. *Create a marketing and sales strategy*: Develop a plan for how you will attract and retain customers, such as through social media, email marketing, and search engine optimization.

5. *Outline your operational plan*: Describe how you will handle day-to-day operations, such as order fulfillment and customer service.

6. *Financial projections*: Create financial projections for the first few years of your business, including projected income, expenses, and profitability.

7. *Include an executive summary*: A brief summary of the business plan that highlights the main points and the purpose of the plan.

8. *Get feedback*: Share your plan with others and get feedback, this can help you spot any errors or areas that need more work.

A good business plan should be clear, concise and provide a roadmap to achieve the business goals. A business plan is not only a tool for fundraising but also a management tool that helps you to focus on the key elements of your business and make better decisions.

Tools to help you build a business plan

There are several tools available to help you build a business plan for your dropshipping business, including:

1. *Business plan templates*: Many online resources such as SCORE, Bplans, and SBA provide business plan templates that you can use as a starting point. These templates provide a structure and guide for creating a business plan.

2. *Business plan software*: There are a variety of software programs such as LivePlan, Business Plan Pro, and Enloop that offer step-by-step guidance and templates for creating a business plan.

3. *Financial planning tools*: Tools such as PlanGuru, TillerHQ, and ProjectionHub, can help you create detailed financial projections for your business plan.

4.   *Online business plan builders*: Platforms like Upmetrics and Enloop offer online business plan builders that help you create professional business plans with step-by-step guidance.

5.   *Mind mapping tools*: Software like MindNode, Xmind, and MindMeister can help you organize your ideas and create a visual representation of your business plan.

A business plan is a living document and should be reviewed and updated regularly as your business evolves. While these tools can be very helpful, they are not a replacement for a deep understanding of your business, your market and your customers. The most important thing is to have a clear vision of your business, your target market, and your goals.

Successful marketing strategy

A successful marketing strategy is one that effectively promotes a product or service, attracts and retains customers, and ultimately drives sales and revenue growth for a business. How to work out a successful marketing strategy:

1.   *Clear and well-defined target market*: A successful marketing strategy begins by identifying and understanding your target market, including their demographics, needs, and pain points.

2.   *Unique selling proposition (USP)*: Having a unique selling proposition (USP) that differentiates your product or service from your competitors.

3.   *A multi-channel approach*: A successful marketing strategy employs a multi-channel approach that reaches customers across a variety of platforms and touchpoints, such as social media, email, search engines, and offline advertising.

4.   *Data-driven decision making*: A successful marketing strategy relies on data to inform decisions, such as which channels to use, what messaging to use, and when to launch campaigns.

5.   *Continual testing and optimization*: A successful marketing strategy is not set in stone and requires continual testing, monitoring and optimization to improve results.

6.   *Tracking and measuring results*: A successful marketing strategy includes tracking and measuring results to evaluate the effectiveness of the strategy and make adjustments as necessary.

7.   *Aligning with overall business goals*: A successful marketing strategy aligns with the goals of the business and supports the growth of the business.

What works for one business may not work for another, and a successful marketing strategy will vary depending on factors such as the business, the product or service, and the target market. A successful marketing strategy is a continuous process that requires regular monitoring, analysis and adjustments.

Strategy tools

There are also other tools that you can use for testing, optimization and project management to help you execute a successful marketing strategy for your dropshipping business, including:

1.　*A/B testing and optimization tools*: Optimizely, VWO, and Google Optimize can help you test and optimize your website and campaigns for better performance.

2.　*Project management tools*: Trello, Asana, and Basecamp can help you organize and manage your marketing tasks and campaigns.

The tools listed in this chapter are just a small part of a larger marketing strategy and should be used in conjunction with a deep understanding of your business, your target market and your goals. The most important aspect of any marketing strategy is to have a clear vision of what you want to achieve and how to reach you target audience using the right methods.

Time

The amount of time required to get started with a dropshipping business can vary depending on several factors such as the complexity of the business model, the type of products you're planning to sell, the resources you have available, and your level of experience.

Here are some general steps that are typically involved in starting a dropshipping business:

1.　*Research and planning*: This stage can take anywhere from a few days to several weeks. During this stage, you'll need to research the market, identify your target audience, and choose your niche.

2.   *Setting up an e-commerce platform*: This can take anywhere from a few hours to a couple of days. You'll need to choose an e-commerce platform, such as Shopify or BigCommerce, and set up the basic infrastructure for your website.

3.   *Finding and sourcing products*: This stage can take anywhere from a few days to several weeks. You'll need to research and find suppliers and manufacturers, and source products that align with your niche and target market.

4.   *Setting up payment and shipping options*: This can take a day or two. You'll need to set up payment options for customers, such as PayPal or Stripe, and shipping options that align with your target market.

5.   *Setting up marketing and advertising*: This stage can take anywhere from a few days to several weeks. You'll need to develop a marketing strategy and set up advertising campaigns to attract customers to your website.

6.   *Launch and ongoing maintenance*: Once your site is set up, you can launch your business. A dropshipping business requires ongoing maintenance, including regular product sourcing, marketing, customer service, and financial management.

In general, it can take anywhere from a couple of weeks to several months to get a dropshipping business up and running, depending on the factors mentioned above. A dropshipping business is a continuous process; it requires continual monitoring, analysis, and adjustments.

Shopify statistics and risks

Shopify is a popular e-commerce platform. Businesses can create an online store and sell their products. It is a cloud-based platform that provides users with a variety of tools and features to create and manage an online store, including website building tools, payment processing, inventory management, and shipping integration.

Here are a few steps to help you use Shopify:

1.   *Create an account*: Sign up for a Shopify account and choose a pricing plan that fits your business needs.

2.   *Customize your store*: Use the website building tools to customize the design and layout of your online store.

3.   *Add products*: Add products to your store by creating product listings and uploading images and descriptions.

4.   *Configure payment and shipping options*: Set up payment options such as PayPal, Stripe, and credit card processing. Configure shipping options, such as shipping rates, taxes, and carrier integration.

5.   *Launch your store*: Once your store is set up, you can launch it and start selling products.

6.   *Monitor and manage your store*: Use the analytics and reporting tools to monitor the performance of your store and manage your inventory and orders.

Shopify is considered a good e-commerce platform because it is user-friendly, easy to set up and customize, has a wide range of features and apps, and has a strong customer support team.

Shopify has a large and active community of users who can provide support and resources.

As of 2021, Shopify has over 1.7 million active businesses using the platform, with a total GMV (Gross Merchandise Volume) of over $155 billion. Shopify had over 1.1 billion in revenue in 2020.

As with any platform, there are some risks to using Shopify, such as the cost of using the platform, the risk of hacking or data breaches, and the risk of reliance on a third-party platform. Shopify takes security very seriously and uses industry-standard security measures to keep user data safe. Shopify has a dedicated security team that monitors and updates the platform to keep it secure.

Product research

Finding the right product to sell is a crucial step in starting a successful dropshipping business. Here are a few steps that can help you conduct product research:

1.   *Identify a niche market*: Start by identifying a niche market that interests you or that you have some knowledge about. This could be a specific product category, such as outdoor gear or beauty products, or a specific customer demographic, such as pet owners or new parents.

2.   *Conduct market research*: Use tools like Google Trends, SEMrush, and Ahrefs to research the market, identify customer needs and pain points, and analyze the competition. Look at what

products are currently trending, what customer needs are not being met, and what gaps in the market exist.

3.   *Analyze your competition*: Look at the websites of your competitors and take note of their best-selling products, pricing, and marketing strategies. Identify what they are doing well and what they could be doing better.

4.   *Use "social media listening"*: Utilize social media platforms like Twitter, Instagram, and Facebook to "listen" to customer conversations and identify what products are popular and what customers are looking for.

5.   *Test products*: Once you have a list of potential products, consider testing them on a small scale to see how they perform in the market. This can be done by creating a small campaign or by testing the product with a small group of customers.

6.   *Look for supplier's products*: Look for suppliers or manufacturers that carry the products you are interested in selling.

Keep in mind that product research is a continuous process, as markets and customer needs are constantly changing. It's a good idea to regularly review and update your product research to ensure that you're always offering products that are in demand and align with the needs of your target market.

Good pricing strategy

A good pricing strategy is one that helps a business achieve its goals while remaining competitive in the market. Here are a few elements of a good pricing strategy:

1.   *Cost-plus pricing*: The strategy involves adding a markup to the original price of the product. This is a popular strategy for businesses that have consistent costs and are looking to achieve a certain profit margin.

2.   *Value-based pricing*: This strategy involves setting a price based on the perceived value of the product to the customer, rather than the cost of the product. This strategy is often used for unique or high-end products.

3.   *Competitive pricing*: This strategy involves setting a price based on the prices of similar products in the market. This strategy is often used by businesses that are entering a new market or facing high competition.

4.   *Psychological pricing*: This strategy involves setting prices that take into account the customer's perception of value, such as using odd pricing (e.g. $9.99 instead of $10) or emphasizing discounts or sales.

5.   *Dynamic pricing*: This strategy involves adjusting prices based on real-time market conditions, such as supply and demand, or the prices of competitors.

A good pricing strategy will vary depending on factors such as the business, the product, and the target market. You have to consider the costs of the product, the target market, and the competition when determining the price. A good pricing strategy should be flexible; it can be reviewed and adjusted over time as market conditions change.

Promote your products

Promoting your products is an essential part of running a successful dropshipping business. Here are a few examples of how to promote your products:

1. *Social media marketing*: Use social media platforms like Facebook, Instagram, and Twitter to promote your products and engage with customers. Create a social media strategy that includes regular posts, contests, and promotions.

2. *Email marketing*: Build an email list of customers and use it to send targeted promotional campaigns and special offers.

3. *Influencer marketing*: You can partner up with influencers on Instagram in order to promote your products to their followers.

4. *Content marketing*: Create valuable and informative content that highlights your products and attracts customers to your website.

5. *Paid advertising*: Use paid advertising platforms like Google Ads, Facebook Ads, and Instagram Ads to promote your products and reach a larger audience.

6. *SEO*: Optimize your website and products for search engines to increase your visibility and attract more customers.

7. *Referral marketing*: Encourage customers to share your products with friends and family in exchange for discounts or rewards.

8. *Networking*: Attend relevant trade shows and events, and make connections with other businesses in your industry.

Promoting your products is a continuous process; it requires regular monitoring, analysis, and adjustments. It's important to test and experiment with different promotional methods to see which ones are most effective for your business.

Referral marketing tools

There are several tools available to help you with referral marketing for your dropshipping business. Some popular tools include:

1.   **ReferralCandy**: This tool helps you create and manage referral programs for your business. It allows you to set up referral rewards, track referrals, and automate follow-up emails.

2.   **Referral Rock**: This platform facilitates the creation, monitoring, and administration of referral programs. It helps you to generate tailor-made referral pages, monitor the progress of referrals, and automate the allocation of referral rewards.

3.   **Ambassador Referral**: This platform allows you to create and manage referral, affiliate and influencer programs. It allows you to track and measure the performance of your referral program and automate commission payouts.

4.   **Friendbuy**: This platform helps you create, track and manage referral programs. It allows you to create custom referral pages, track referral progress, and automate referral rewards.

5.   **ReferralHero**: This platform supports the creation, monitoring, and management of referral programs. You can design

personalized referral pages, monitor the progress of referrals, and automate the distribution of referral rewards.

6.   **Post Affiliate Pro**: This platform helps you create, track, and manage referral, affiliate and partner programs. It allows you to track and measure the performance of your referral program, automate commission payouts and create custom landing pages.

Referral marketing can be a powerful way to attract new customers, increase sales and grow your business, but it requires regular monitoring, analysis, and adjustments.

Conclusion

Dropshipping is a business model that allows entrepreneurs to sell products without the need for inventory or warehousing. It's a popular choice for people who want to start an e-commerce business, as it requires less investment and less risk than traditional e-commerce models. Starting a dropshipping business requires a good product research, a clear understanding of the target market, a solid marketing strategy, and a well-designed e-commerce website. It's important to have a good pricing strategy, and a variety of tools are available to help with this.

Starting a dropshipping business is not without its challenges. The market can be very competitive, and you have to stay on top of trends and customer needs. A successful dropshipping business requires ongoing work and maintenance, including regular product sourcing, marketing, customer service, and financial management.

Dropshipping can be a great way to start an e-commerce business, but it's important to do your research, plan carefully, and be prepared for the challenges that come with running a business. With the right approach, a dropshipping business can be a rewarding and profitable venture.

#5

Start A YouTube Channel

YouTube Ventures

Starting a YouTube channel can be a fun and exciting way to share your interests and talents with the world. Here are the some steps to get started:

1.   *Create a Google account*: Before you can start a YouTube channel, you'll need a Google account. If you already have one, you can use it to create your channel. If not, go to the Google sign-up page and create a new account.

2.   *Sign in to YouTube*: Once you have a Google account, go to the YouTube website and sign in. You'll be prompted to create a channel, or you can click on the three lines in the top left corner, select My Channel, and then create a channel.

3.   *Choose a channel name*: Pick a name that represents your brand or something easy to remember, it could be your name or a business name.

4.   *Customize your channel*: Now that your channel is set up, you can add a profile picture, banner, and other information that will help your viewers understand what your channel is about.

5.   *Create content*: The most important part of a YouTube channel is the content. You'll need to create and upload videos to your channel. You can use a camera or smartphone to record your

videos or use screen recording software to create videos from your computer.

Why YouTube?

YouTube is a popular platform that can be a great way to make money. Here are a few reasons why:

1.   *Large audience*: YouTube is the *second-largest search engine* in the world and has over 2 billion monthly active users. This means that your videos have the potential to reach a large audience, giving you the opportunity to make money from a variety of sources.

2.   *Advertising revenue*: One way to make money on YouTube is through advertising. You can monetize your videos and earn money from ads that are displayed on them. The more views your videos get, the more money you can earn.

3.   *Sponsorships and collaborations*: As your channel grows, you may also be able to secure sponsorships and collaborations with brands. These partnerships can be a great way to earn money while also promoting products or services that align with your channel's content.

4.   *Product sales and services*: Having a large audience gives you the opportunity to promote your own products, such as e-books, courses, or merchandise. Many YouTubers make a significant amount of money by *selling their own products* on their channel.

5.   *YouTube Premium*: YouTube has a premium service called YouTube Premium, where users pay a monthly fee for an ad-free experience and access to exclusive content. You can earn money from users watching your content on YouTube Premium.

YouTube offers a lot of ways to monetize your content and make money, but it takes time, effort, and consistency. It will not happen overnight, but with consistent effort, you can build a sizable audience and income stream through the platform.

Is YouTube for you?

YouTube is a platform that can be ideal for a wide range of people, including:

1.   *Creators*: YouTube is ideal for creators of all types, such as vloggers, gamers, comedians, musicians, educators, and more. It's a platform where anyone can share their creativity and passion with the world.

2.   *Entrepreneurs*: YouTube is a great platform for entrepreneurs and small business owners to build an audience and promote their products and services. It allows them to create video content to share their knowledge and build trust with their audience.

3.   *Influencers*: YouTube can be a great platform for influencers to share their expertise and experiences with a large audience, allowing them to build a community of loyal fans and make money from sponsored content and affiliate marketing.

4. *Educators*: YouTube is a powerful platform for educators. Many teachers and trainers use YouTube to share their knowledge and provide a valuable resource for students, by creating videos that explain complex concepts, show how to solve problems, or demonstrate practical skills.

5. *Entertainers*: YouTube is a great platform for entertainers to share their talents and showcase their performances to a global audience. Musicians, comedians, and other entertainers can use YouTube to reach new fans and build their careers.

YouTube isn't just ideal for these groups, many people use YouTube for personal expression, entertainment, education, and even as a platform to promote their businesses or showcase their talents. The versatility of YouTube allows individuals from all walks of life to find their place and connect with others who share their interests. Whether you're a filmmaker, a musician, a beauty enthusiast, a fitness guru, or simply someone with a unique perspective to share, YouTube offers a space for you to be seen, heard, and celebrated. It is a vibrant community that welcomes diversity, fosters creativity, and provides endless possibilities for anyone willing to embark on the YouTube journey.

Skillset

Here are some skills that can be helpful when starting a YouTube channel:

1. *Creativity*: The ability to come up with interesting and engaging ideas for your videos is essential for success on YouTube. It's also important to be able to think outside the box and stand out from the crowd. To research ideas and topics you can

also use ChatGPT, it help you brainstorm ideas and come up with catchy and unique titles for your videos.

2.   *Video production and editing*: Basic video production and editing skills can help you create videos that are high-quality, visually appealing, and easy to watch. You don't need to have advanced skills, but knowing how to use the basic features of video editing software, like cutting, splicing, and adding music, can be helpful.

3.   *Audio production*: Audio quality is also important. You may want to learn some basics of audio recording and editing to make sure that your videos sound clear and professional.

4.   *Writing and storytelling*: Being able to write compelling scripts or captions and tells a story through your videos can help you connect with your audience and keep them engaged. This is another point where you can use ChatGPT for help.

5.   *Marketing*: Understanding how to promote and market your channel is important for growing your audience and making money. Marketing skills will help you *attract and retain* viewers.

6.   *Patience and consistency*: Success on YouTube takes time, and most important is to be consistent and patient in building your channel. It can be helpful to develop a content calendar and stick to a regular posting schedule. In some cases you might need to have uploaded at least 50-60 videos to your channel, before you start seeing some real engagement.

You don't need to have all these skills but having some knowledge in these areas can help you create a more polished and professional channel. As you gain more experience and grow your channel, you can learn new skills and improve on existing ones.

Investment

The amount of money you'll need to invest to start a YouTube channel can vary greatly depending on a number of factors, such as the type of equipment you use and the scale of your production.

Starting a YouTube channel is not expensive. You can create content using just a smartphone and a tripod, which can be purchased for a relatively low cost. If you want to produce high-quality videos, then you may need to invest in more expensive equipment, such as camera, lighting, and audio equipment.

Editing software can range from free options like iMovie or OpenShot, to paid options like Adobe Premiere Pro.

Aside from equipment, you may also want to invest in a good internet connection or graphic design software for thumbnails and channel art.

The amount of money you'll need to invest to start a YouTube channel will depend on your goals and the type of content you plan to create. You can start small and gradually invest more as you grow your channel and gain more income.

Have in mind, that while it's possible to make money on YouTube, it's not guaranteed and you should be prepared to invest time and resources to grow your channel. Be sure to have realistic expectations and consider how you plan to monetize your channel before you start.

Time

The amount of time it takes to start a YouTube channel can vary depending on a number of factors, such as the type of content you plan to create and your skills.

Some of the tasks that you'll need to complete before starting your channel include:

1.   *Researching your niche and identifying your target audience*: This can take anywhere from a few hours to a few days, depending on how thorough your research is.

2.   *Setting up your channel*: Creating your channel, designing your profile and channel art, and adding information about your channel can take a few hours to a day; depending on how detailed you want your channel to be.

3.   *Preparing your content*: Preparing your first few videos, planning your content calendar, scripting, filming, and editing can take a significant amount of time, depending on how complicated your content is.

4.   *Promoting your channel*: After you've created your channel and posted a few videos, you'll need to promote it to attract viewers. This can take a few days to a few weeks, depending on how much effort you put into it.

It is difficult to estimate the exact time required to get started as it largely depends on your goals and schedule. Some people may be able to get their channel up and running in a few days, while others may take longer. Starting a YouTube channel is also a long-term commitment, regular posting, and engagement will be necessary to maintain and grow your audience over time.

Topics

Finding topics that you're interested in is an important step in starting a YouTube channel. Here are a few tips to help you find topics that you're passionate about:

1.   *Think about your hobbies and interests*: What are the things that you enjoy doing in your free time? Whether it's playing video games, cooking, doing DIY projects, or something else, these interests can often make great topics for videos.

2.   *Recognize your areas of expertise and talents*: What abilities and skills do you possess? Whether you have a talent for drawing, writing, photography, or teaching, your strengths can also make great video topics.

3.   *Look for problems to solve*: Many of the most popular YouTube channels focus on solving problems for their viewers. Think about the common questions and issues that people have in your field of interest, and consider how you can help them solve them.

4.   *Pay attention to current events and trends*: Keeping up with the latest events and trends can help you come up with new and interesting video ideas. It can also help you create content that will appeal to a wide range of viewers.

5.   *Try different things*: Experiment with different types of videos, and see what resonates with your audience. You may not hit the jackpot with your first idea, but by experimenting with different styles and formats, you can find the right niche that suits your interests, skills, and personality.

Starting a YouTube channel is a long-term commitment, so you have to pick a topic that you are genuinely interested in and can see yourself creating content for in the long term.

Topic examples

Here's a list of examples of different topics that could make great YouTube channels:

1. **Gaming**: Reviews and walkthroughs of the latest video games, as well as tips and tricks for playing them.

2. **Food**: Cooking and recipe videos, as well as videos about different cuisines and food-related travel experiences.

3. **Fitness and health**: Workout tutorials, healthy living tips, and nutritional advice.

4. **DIY and home improvement**: How-to videos on various projects, such as home repairs, gardening, and crafts.

5. **Technology**: Unboxing, reviews, and tips for the latest gadgets, and technology news updates.

6. **Fashion and beauty**: Makeup tutorials, fashion reviews, and styling tips for different occasions and seasons.

7. **Travel**: Videos about different travel destinations, as well as tips for planning and budgeting for trips.

8. **Education**: Explanations and demonstrations of various academic subjects, as well as study tips and test-taking strategies.

9. **Comedy and entertainment**: Sketch comedy, parodies, and other comedic videos, as well as music videos and other forms of entertainment.

10. **Personal development**: Motivation, productivity, and life-coaching videos that help people to improve their personal and professional lives.

There are many other topics out there, and new topics constantly arising as the world changes. The key is to think about your interests, skills, and passions and how they align with what your target audience might be interested in.

Research

Making *detailed research* about your niche is an important step in starting a YouTube channel and ensuring its success. Here are a few ways to do research about your niche:

1. *Study the competition*: Look at other popular YouTube channels in your niche and see what kind of content they're creating, how they're presenting it, and what their audience is responding to. You can also look at the number of subscribers and views they have, which can give you an idea of how big the audience is in your niche.

2. *Analyze search data*: Use tools like Google Trends, YouTube Search, and Keyword Planner to identify popular keywords and search phrases in your niche. This can give you an idea of what people are looking for when they search for content related to your niche.

3.   *Look at the comments*: Read through the comments on the videos of popular channels in your niche. This can give you an idea of what people are saying about the content and what they want to see more of. It can also give you an insight into the audience demographics and their interest points.

4.   *Monitor social media*: Follow popular accounts on social media that are related to your niche. This can give you an idea of what people are talking about and what types of content are resonating with them.

5.   *Conduct surveys and focus groups*: Ask potential viewers about their interests, problems, and the kind of content they would like to see. This can help you to identify unmet needs and opportunities in your niche.

6.   *Experiment*: Experiment with different types of videos and content formats, and see what resonates with your audience. Then, you can use this feedback to create more targeted and effective content.

Researching your niche takes time and effort, but it will give you a better understanding of your audience and help you to create content that they will love. This will help you to build a more loyal and engaged audience over time.

Gap analysis

Gap analysis is a technique that can be used to identify the difference between where you are and where you want to be in terms of your YouTube channel's performance. Here's how to use gap analysis for your videos:

1.   *Identify your goals*: Clearly define what you want to achieve with your YouTube channel, such as increasing views, subscribers, or revenue.

2.   *Assess your current performance*: Look at your current metrics such as views, subscribers, engagement rate, etc., and compare them to your goals. This will give you a sense of where you currently stand.

3.   *Identify the gaps*: Compare your current performance with your goals and identify the gaps that exist. This will provide insight into areas where you can further enhance your abilities.

4.   *Analyze the reasons for the gaps*: Identify the reasons behind the gaps, such as lack of audience engagement, poor video quality, or inconsistent posting schedule.

5.   *Create a plan of action*: Once you have identified the gaps and the reasons behind them, you can create a plan of action to address them. This may include improving your video quality, increasing your posting frequency, or focusing on more audience-engaging content.

6.   *Implement the plan*: Follow through with the actions outlined in your plan and track your progress.

7.   *Evaluate and adjust*: Continuously evaluate your progress and adjust your plan as needed. Keep track of what works and what doesn't, and adjust your strategy accordingly.

Gap analysis can be a valuable tool for identifying areas where you can improve your YouTube channel, and for developing a plan to help you reach your goals. It can also help you to focus on the most important aspects and track progress over time.

Video thumbnails

Creating great thumbnails and titles for your videos can help to attract more views and make your videos stand out on YouTube. Here are a few tips for creating great thumbnails and titles for your videos:

1.   *Use eye-catching images*: Your thumbnail should be visually compelling and grab the viewer's attention. Use high-resolution images and make sure they are relevant to your video.

2.   *Use text sparingly*: Keep your thumbnail simple and uncluttered. Use text sparingly and make sure it is easy to read and relevant to your video.

3.   *Use colors that stand out*: Use colors that will make your thumbnail stand out against the other thumbnails on YouTube.

4.   *Optimize for different devices*: Make sure your thumbnail looks good on different devices, including smartphones, tablets, and desktops.

5.   *Use clear and concise titles*: Your title should be clear and concise, and it should give viewers an idea of what your video is about. Avoid clickbait titles that may lead to disappointment and a high bounce rate.

6.   *Use keywords*: Use keywords that are relevant to your video in your title, as this will help your video to show up in search results.

7.   *Test different thumbnails and titles*: Test different thumbnails and titles for your videos and see which ones perform the best.

The thumbnail and title are the first things people will see when they come across your video. Having an attention-grabbing and clear thumbnail and title can be the difference in getting clicks and views. Experiment with different styles and make adjustments as you gain more data about your audience.

Increase your video engagement

Increasing engagement on your videos is important for growing your YouTube channel and keeping your audience interested. Here are a few ways to increase engagement on your videos:

1.   *Create compelling content*: Create videos that are interesting, informative, and engaging. Consider using storytelling techniques and make sure that your videos are well-produced and edited.

2.   *Engage with your audience*: Respond to comments on your videos, and encourage your audience to leave comments, feedback, or questions. You can also use polls or quizzes to engage with your audience and get their opinion on different topics.

3.   *Promote your videos*: Share your videos on social media and other platforms to increase visibility and reach a wider audience.

4.   *Collaborate with other YouTubers*: Collaborating with other YouTubers can help you reach a wider audience and increase engagement on your videos. This can be done by featuring other YouTubers in your videos or by doing a video together.

5.   *Use subtitles and closed captions*: Subtitles and closed captions are a great way to increase engagement; they make your videos accessible to a wider audience, including individuals with hearing impairments, and those who come from diverse linguistic backgrounds.

6.   *Utilize YouTube features*: Use YouTube features like end screens, and cards to encourage viewers to watch more of your videos, and to subscribe to your channel.

7.   *Engage with your community*: Building a strong community on YouTube takes time, but you can do it by responding to comments, creating a community tab on your channel, and working on regular interaction with your viewers.

Increasing engagement on your videos is a long-term effort. It takes time, consistency, and effort to grow an engaged audience. Use analytics to track your progress and make adjustments as needed.

Promotion

Promoting your videos is an important step in growing your YouTube channel and reaching a wider audience. Here are a few ways to promote your videos:

1.   *Share on social media*: Share your videos on your social media accounts like Facebook, Twitter, Instagram, etc. This will help to increase visibility and reach a wider audience.

2.   *Use email marketing*: Share your videos with your email subscribers by including them in your newsletter or by sending a dedicated email.

3.   *Embed on your website*: Embed your videos on your website or blog to increase visibility and drive traffic to your YouTube channel.

4.   *Optimize for search*: Optimize your video descriptions and titles for search using relevant keywords. This will help your videos to show up in search results when people are searching for content related to your niche.

5.   *Advertise*: Invest in advertising, such as Google AdWords or YouTube Ads, to reach a larger audience.

6.   *Create Playlists*: Create playlists of your videos on your channel. This will make it easier for viewers to find all your videos on related topics, and also increase your video's visibility.

7.   *Use call-to-action*: End your videos with a call-to-action, such as asking viewers to subscribe, watch another video, or leave a comment.

The key to promoting your videos is consistency, and always keep experimenting with different strategies to see which one is the most effective for your channel and audience. Also, it is important to engage with your audience and create a relationship with them, this will increase the chances that they will share and promote your content.

SEO Optimization

Search Engine Optimization (SEO) is an important aspect of promoting your YouTube channel, and reaching a wider audience. Here are a few tips for doing SEO correctly for your YouTube videos:

1.   *Optimize your video title*: Use a title that includes relevant keywords for your video and make sure it accurately describes the content of the video.

2.   *Optimize your video description*: Use a description that includes relevant keywords and gives a brief overview of the video's content. Include a link to your website or other relevant links if applicable.

3.   *Use tags*: Add relevant tags to your video to help it show up in search results for those specific keywords.

4.   *Create transcripts*: YouTube allows you to add transcripts of your videos; it will increase its accessibility and will make it easier for search engines to understand the content of your video.

5.   *Optimize your video thumbnail*: Use an engaging and relevant thumbnail that accurately represents your video.

6.   *Optimize your video's file name*: Rename your video file to include relevant keywords and keep it short and easy to remember.

7.   *Optimize your video's metadata*: Use YouTube's built-in video metadata editor to add information about your video such as its title, description, and tags.

8.   *Create a video sitemap*: Create a sitemap for your videos and submit it to Google to make sure that all your videos get indexed by the search engines. *

9.   *Get backlinks*: Get backlinks to your YouTube channel from other websites. The more backlinks your channel has the higher it will rank on search results.

10.   *Regularly upload videos*: The more frequently you upload videos, the more opportunities you have to engage with your audience, build a loyal following, and increase your visibility in the YouTube community.

*Create a sitemap for your videos and submit it to Google

To create a video sitemap and submit it to Google, you can follow these steps:

Generate a video sitemap: You can manually create a video sitemap using XML markup or use online tools or plugins that can help you generate a sitemap automatically. Ensure that the sitemap includes relevant information about each video, such as the video URL, title, description, duration, and thumbnail URL.

Validate your video sitemap: Use a sitemap validation tool, such as the Google Search Console's Sitemaps report, to validate your video sitemap. This step helps identify any errors or issues that need to be addressed before submission.

Upload your video sitemap to your website: Place the video sitemap file in the root directory of your website or the specific location recommended by your content management system

(CMS). Ensure that the sitemap file is accessible and properly linked within your website's structure.

Sign in to Google Search Console: Access your Google Search Console account or create one if you don't have it already.

Add your website property: In the Google Search Console dashboard, click on "Add Property" and enter the URL of your website. Follow the verification process to confirm ownership of the website.

Submit your video sitemap: Under the "Sitemaps" section in Google Search Console, enter the URL of your video sitemap and click on "Submit." Google will then fetch the sitemap and process the video URLs within it.

Monitor indexing status: Check the indexing status of your video URLs in Google Search Console. This will give you insights into how Google is processing and including your videos in search results.

Remember to keep your video sitemap up to date by adding new videos or removing out-dated ones as your content library evolves. Regularly check Google Search Console for any potential issues or notifications related to your video sitemap and addresses them promptly.

Please note that while submitting a video sitemap can improve the visibility of your videos in Google search results, it does not guarantee immediate or guaranteed inclusion. Google's algorithms determine the ranking and visibility of your videos based on various factors, including relevance, quality, and user engagement.

Monetization

Setting up monetization on your YouTube channel allows you to earn money from your videos through ads, sponsorships, and other revenue streams. Here's how to set up monetization for your YouTube channel:

1.   *Meet YouTube's Partner Program requirements*: To monetize your videos, your channel must meet YouTube's Partner Program requirements. These requirements entail having a minimum of 1,000 subscribers and accumulating 4,000 watch hours within the past 12 months. You will also need to comply with YouTube's community guidelines and terms of service.

2.   *Create a Google AdSense account*: In order to monetize your videos, you will need to have a Google AdSense account. This is the platform that YouTube uses to pay its partners. If you haven't created an AdSense account yet, you can easily sign up for one directly through the YouTube Studio.

3.   *Link your AdSense account to your YouTube channel*: Once you have created an AdSense account, you will need to link it to your YouTube channel. This can be done through the Monetization tab in YouTube Studio.

4.   *Set up monetization for your videos*: Once your AdSense account is linked, you can set up monetization for your videos. Go to the Monetization tab in YouTube Studio and select the videos that you want to monetize. You will then be prompted to review and accept YouTube's monetization terms.

5.   *Select monetization options*: After you have set up monetization for your videos, you can select which monetization options you want to enable. This can include ads, sponsorships, or

other revenue streams such as merchandise or membership programs.

6.   *Customize ad settings*: You can also customize your ad settings in the Monetization tab. This includes choosing which ad formats to display, such as skippable ads or non-skippable ads, and setting a filter for sensitive content.

7.   *Keep in mind the terms of service*: YouTube's terms of service and guidelines change frequently so keep in mind to review them often to make sure that your videos comply with them and your monetization won't be affected.

Monetization takes time to set up and it might take some time before you start seeing revenues, but once you have it set up, it can be a good source of income for your channel. Remember that to make significant revenue, you'll need a large number of views and a consistent, engaged audience.

Conclusion

Starting a YouTube channel opens up a world of opportunities. It allows you to share your passions, creativity, and knowledge with a global audience. Through your videos, you can connect with like-minded individuals, build a community, and make a positive impact on the lives of others.

One of the greatest benefits of starting a YouTube channel is the ability to express yourself authentically. You have the freedom to create content that reflects your unique voice, style, and perspective. Whether you're sharing tutorials, vlogs, entertainment, or educational content, your channel becomes a canvas for your creativity.

Beyond self-expression, a YouTube channel offers the potential for personal growth and development. As you create and refine your content, you'll hone your storytelling, communication, and video editing skills. You'll learn to adapt to changing trends and technologies, pushing yourself to stay ahead in a dynamic digital landscape.

Moreover, a successful YouTube channel can provide financial rewards. Through monetization, partnerships, and sponsorships, you can turn your passion into a sustainable income stream. While it may take time and dedication to reach significant financial milestones, the potential is there for those who are willing to put in the effort.

But perhaps the most rewarding aspect of starting a YouTube channel is the impact you can have on others. Your videos can entertain, inspire, educate, and even bring comfort to people around the world. The comments and messages from viewers who have found value in your content are a testament to the difference you can make in their lives.

The journey of a YouTube creator is not without challenges. It requires dedication, consistency, and the ability to adapt to a constantly evolving platform. Building an audience takes time and effort, and setbacks are a part of the process. The rewards of connecting with a supportive community and leaving a lasting legacy make it all worthwhile.

As you embark on your own YouTube journey, embrace the opportunities, learn from the setbacks, and keep pushing forward. The possibilities are limitless, and your channel has the power to make a difference in ways you may never have imagined.

Go forth and create. The world is waiting to hear your story, see your talent, and be inspired by your unique perspective. Good luck in the incredible world of YouTube, where creativity knows no bounds!

#6

Product comparison websites

Compare and Profit

A product comparison website is a type of e-commerce website that allows users to compare different products, typically in the same category, based on specific features and attributes. The website may also provide information on pricing and where to purchase the products. The main reason to create a product comparison website is to help users find the best product for their needs and budget by providing them with all the information they need in one place. Users would go to your website to save time and energy in their product research by having a single source of information, also they would trust your website as a unbiased source that is not trying to sell them one product over the other.

How to make money

A product comparison website can be a good way to make money, but it depends on the specific business model and how it is executed. Some common ways that product comparison websites make money include:

• **Affiliate marketing**: The website earns a commission when users click on links to purchase products on other websites.

• **Advertising**: The website earns money by displaying ads from other companies.

• **Sponsored content**: The website earns money by featuring sponsored products or reviews.

• **Lead generation**: The website earns money by collecting leads (e.g. contact information) from users who are interested in purchasing products.

Note that creating a successful product comparison website can be a significant undertaking, as it requires a significant investment in time, resources, and expertise. The competition in this space can be intense and it requires a lot of effort to make it profitable. You have to have a well-defined target audience, a clear business model, a solid SEO strategy and a marketing plan.

The process of getting started

Here are some general steps to get you started with creating a product comparison website:

1. *Define your niche*: Identify a specific product category or niche that you want to focus on. This will help you to target a specific audience and make it easier for you to gather and organize information about the products you will be comparing. Some things to consider when defining your niche include:

• **Popularity**: Choose a product category that is in high demand and has a large potential customer base.

• **Competitors**: Research the competition in your chosen niche to see what they are doing well and what areas they could improve upon.

• **Expertise**: Choose a niche that you are passionate about and have some level of expertise in. This will make it easier for you to gather and organize information about the products you will be comparing.

• **Profit potential**: Consider the profit potential of the niche, this means, the potential to monetize it by using affiliate marketing, advertising, sponsored content, or lead generation.

Once you have a clear idea of what niche you want to focus on, you can start gathering information about the products you want to include on your website and start building your website. Remember that the niche you choose can affect the monetization strategy, so it's important to have a clear idea of how you want to monetize it.

2. *Research your competition*: Look at other product comparison websites in your niche. Which products are performing well and what could be improved? This will help you understand the market and identify opportunities for your own website. Here are some things to consider when researching your competition:

• **Website design**: Look at the design and layout of your competitors' websites. Take note of what is effective and areas that may benefit from change and improvement.

•   **Content**: Look at the type of content that your competitors are providing. This could include product reviews, buying guides, and other types of informational content.

•   **Product selection**: Look at the products that your competitors are featuring on their website. This will give you an idea of what products are popular in your niche and which ones you should consider featuring on your own website.

•   **Monetization strategy**: Look at how your competitors are monetizing their website. This could include affiliate marketing, advertising, sponsored content, or lead generation.

•   **SEO**: Check their SEO strategy, for example, how they are using keywords, meta tags, and backlinks. This will help you understand how to optimize your own website for search engines.

By researching your competition, you can get a better understanding of what works well in your niche and what areas you can improve upon. This can help you to create a website that stands out from the competition and attracts more users.

3.   *Gather product information*: Collect information on the products you want to include on your website. This may include things like product features, prices, and customer reviews. Here are some things to consider when gathering product information:

•   **Product features**: Collect information on the different features of each product, such as size, weight, color options, warranty, and any other relevant information that users may be interested in.

• **Prices**: Collect information on the prices of each product, including any sales or discounts that may be available.

• **Customer reviews**: Look for customer reviews of each product. This will give you an idea of what users like and dislike about each product and can help you to create more accurate product reviews.

• **Product images**: Collect high-quality images of each product, as this will make your website more visually appealing and help users to get a better idea of what each product looks like.

• **Product availability**: Check the availability of each product, if it's in stock or out of stock, also check where it can be purchased.

By gathering this information, you can create a comprehensive product comparison page that will provide users with all the information they need to make an informed purchasing decision. Keep in mind that to keep your website updated, you will need to check for new products, new features and new prices regularly, and to have a system to update all this information automatically.

4.   *Build your website*: Use a website builder or hire a web developer to create your website. What is important is that the website it is user-friendly and easy to navigate. Here are some things to consider when building your website:

• **Platform**: Take your time and make proper research before you choose a platform. Some website builders Wix or Squarespace are a good point to start. Another option is to hire a web designer who can design a website tailored to your needs.

•	**Design**: Make sure that your website is visually appealing and easy to navigate. Use a clean, modern design that is easy on the eyes and easy to use.

•	**User experience**: The website has to be easy to use. This includes things like intuitive navigation, clear calls to action, and simple forms.

•	**Speed**: Make sure that your website loads quickly, this is important for user experience, SEO and for a good ranking on search engines.

•	**Mobile-friendly**: Ensure that your website is mobile-friendly and responsive, this means that it can be easily viewed and navigated on different devices and screen sizes.

•	**Security**: Make sure that your website is secure, this means that it should have an SSL certificate and regularly update the software, to avoid vulnerabilities and hacking.

•	**Integration**: Consider integrating your website with other tools, such as Google Analytics, to help you track website traffic, user behavior and optimize your website accordingly.

By building a well-designed and user-friendly website, you can provide your users with an enjoyable and informative experience that will keep them coming back.

5.	*Create content*: Creating high-quality, informative content is important for building a successful product comparison website.

By writing product reviews, guides, and other content that is useful to your target audience, you can provide them with the information they need to make informed purchasing decisions. Here are some things to consider when creating content for your product comparison website:

• **Product reviews**: Write detailed, unbiased reviews of the products you are featuring on your website. Include information on the product's features, pros and cons, and how it compares to similar products.

• **Buying guides**: Write guides that help users understand the different features and attributes of different products and how to choose the best one for their needs.

• **How-to articles**: Write articles that provide step-by-step instructions on how to use or maintain different products.

• **News and updates**: Keep your audience updated on the latest news and developments in your niche, such as new product releases, price changes, and other relevant information.

• **User-generated content**: Encourage your users to share their own reviews and experiences with different products. This can help to build trust and credibility for your website.

• **Optimize for SEO**: Optimize your content for search engines by including relevant keywords, meta tags, and backlinks.

• **Engage with your audience**: Respond to comments and questions from your audience, this will help to build trust and engagement.

By providing high-quality, informative content that is useful to your target audience, you can increase the chances that they will return to your website and trust your recommendations. Make sure that your content is well-organized, easy to read, and visually appealing, this will help keep your users engaged and interested in your website.

6.   *Optimize for SEO*: Optimizing your website and content for search engines is an important step in building a successful product comparison website. By optimizing your website for search engines, you can increase your website's visibility, attract more traffic, and ultimately, help your website to be easily found by users. Here are some things to consider when optimizing your website and content for search engines:

•   **Keyword research**: Research keywords that are relevant to your niche and include them in your website's content, meta tags, and URLs.

•   **On-page optimization**: Optimize your website's on-page elements, such as title tags, meta descriptions, header tags, and alt tags, to make them more search engine friendly.

•   **Content optimization**: Optimize your website's content by including relevant keywords, internal linking, and meta tags.

•   **Technical optimization**: Optimize your website's technical elements, such as site speed, mobile responsiveness, and website structure, to make it more search engine friendly.

- **Link building**: Obtain backlinks from other websites to your website, this will help to increase your website's domain authority and improve its search engine rankings.

- **Use of structured data**: Use structured data to mark up your website's content, this will help search engines understand the content of your website and display it in a more meaningful way to the users.

- **Tracking your progress**: Use tools like Google Analytics to track your website's search engine performance and identify areas for improvement.

By optimizing your website and content for search engines, you can improve your website's visibility, attract more traffic and make it more easily found by users. SEO is a continuous process, and you have to stay up to date with the latest SEO best practices and algorithm updates.

7. *Promote your website*: Promoting your website is an important step in building a successful product comparison website. By promoting your website, you can generate traffic, attract users, and ultimately increase your website's visibility and revenue potential.

- **Social media**: Share your website on different social media platforms, such as Facebook, Instagram, Twitter, and LinkedIn. This can help to increase your website's visibility and attract more users.

- **Online forums**: Participate in online forums that are relevant to your niche, such as product review forums, and share your website with other users.

- **Influencer marketing**: You can use influencers to promote your website to their followers.

- **Content marketing**: Create and share high-quality content, such as blog posts, infographics, and videos, that can help to attract users to your website.

- **Email marketing**: Build an email list and send out regular newsletters to keep users informed about new products, updates, and promotions on your website.

- **Paid advertising**: Consider using paid advertising, such as Google Adwords, to attract more users to your website.

- **Referral marketing**: Encourage your existing users to refer their friends and family to your website.

- **Public relations**: Reach out to media outlets and publications in your niche and ask them to feature your website.

By promoting your website, you can generate traffic, attract users, and ultimately increase your website's visibility and revenue potential. It's important to have a well-defined target audience, a clear marketing strategy, and to track and measure the results, to adjust your strategy accordingly.

8. *Monetize your website*: Monetizing your website is an important step in creating a sustainable product comparison website. By monetizing your website, you can generate revenue

and make your website financially viable. Here are few strategies to have in mind:

• **Affiliate marketing**: This is a revenue-sharing model where you include affiliate links to products on your website and earn a commission when users click on those links and make a purchase. You always need to have a disclaimer and inform your customers that you may earn a comission when using your link. Refer to Chapter #10 Affiliate Marketing: *Earnings Unleashed* on page 147.

• **Advertising**: You can place ads on your website and earn money through pay-per-click (PPC) or cost-per-thousand-impressions (CPM) models.

• **Sponsored content**: You can create sponsored content, such as sponsored product reviews or sponsored blog posts, and earn money from the advertiser.

• **Lead generation**: You can collect leads from users who are interested in purchasing products and sell them to companies or earn commissions from them.

• **Subscription model**: You can offer premium features and exclusive content for users who subscribe to your website.

• **E-commerce**: You can sell your own products or digital goods, such as e-books or courses.

Not all monetization strategies will work for every website and it's crucial to find the one that fits best with your niche, target audience, and overall business model. You have to implement these strategies in a way that doesn't compromise the user experience or damage the trust of your audience.

Build a website without budget

Building a product comparison website without any budget can be challenging, but it is possible. Here are few ideas on how to start:

1.   *Use a free website builder*: There are several website builders, such as Wix or Weebly, that offer free plans that you can use to create a basic website. These plans typically have limitations, such as limited storage and bandwidth, but they can be a good option if you don't have a budget.

2.   *Use a free Content Management System (CMS):* Use a free CMS such as WordPress, to build your website. WordPress is open-source, meaning it's free to use, but you would need to pay for web hosting and a domain name.

3.   *Use Open-source e-commerce platform*: Some open-source e-commerce platforms like OpenCart, or PrestaShop can be used to create a product comparison website. They are free to use, but they require web hosting and a domain name, also, they might require some technical skills to set it up and customize it.

4.   *Gather product information manually*: Instead of using a paid data feed or API to gather product information, manually gather the information by visiting different e-commerce websites and collecting the information you need.

5.   *Use free images and icons*: Use free stock images and icons to make your website more visually appealing. There are several websites, such as Unsplash, Pexels, or Icons8, that offer free high-quality images and icons.

6.   *Use free tools for SEO and analytics*: Use free tools like Google Analytics to track website traffic and user behavior. Also, use free SEO tools like Search Console Insights, to check your website's performance and identify areas for improvement.

Building a product comparison website without a budget may require more time, effort, and creativity, but it's possible. You must have a solid plan and a clear idea of how you want to monetize it, since the lack of budget can make it harder to monetize your website.

Conclusion

Creating a product comparison website can be a rewarding endeavor, providing valuable information and assistance to users in their purchasing decisions. By following the steps outlined, including defining your niche, researching the competition, gathering product information, building a user-friendly website, creating informative content, optimizing for search engines, promoting your website, and implementing effective monetization strategies, you can increase the chances of building a successful and profitable product comparison website. It's important to approach this endeavor with careful planning, ongoing effort, and adaptability to meet the evolving needs of your target audience and the competitive landscape. By doing so, you can create a valuable resource that serves your users while also generating revenue and growing your online presence.

#7

Video Courses On Udemy

Teaching Online

Creating an online video course on Udemy can be a great way to share your knowledge and expertise with a wide audience. Udemy is an online learning platform that offers courses on a wide range of subjects, from programming and design to personal development and business. By creating a course on Udemy, you have the opportunity to reach thousands of students from all over the world and make a positive impact on their lives. Creating a course can also be a great way to build your personal brand, establish yourself as an expert in your field, and generate additional income. Creating an online video course on Udemy is a great way to share your knowledge, connect with students, and grow your personal and professional brand.

Is this for you?

Creating an online video course on Udemy is ideal for anyone who has knowledge or expertise in a specific subject and wants to share it with a wide audience. This can include:

•   Professionals or experts in a particular field who want to share their knowledge and experience with others

•   Educators or trainers who want to reach a larger audience and supplement their income

• Entrepreneurs or business owners who want to establish themselves as thought leaders in their industry

• Anyone with a passion for a subject and a desire to share that passion with others

It is ideal for people who are looking to earn money by sharing their knowledge. Udemy is a great platform for people who want to monetize their expertise by creating online courses and making passive income.

Creating an online video course on Udemy is ideal for anyone who has knowledge or expertise in a specific subject and wants to share it with others, whether for personal or financial gain.

Skillset

Creating an online video course on Udemy requires several skills:

1. *Subject matter expertise*: You need to have a deep understanding of the subject you are teaching in order to create a comprehensive and accurate course.

2. *Teaching ability*: You should be able to explain complex concepts in an easy-to-understand way, and be able to engage and motivate your students.

3. *Video production skills*: You will need to be able to record and edit high-quality videos that are visually engaging and easy to follow.

4.   *Technical proficiency*: You should have a basic understanding of the technical aspects of creating an online course, such as creating slideshows and downloading videos.

5.   *Marketing and promotion*: You will need to be able to promote your course effectively to reach your target audience and generate sales.

6.   *Patience and persistence*: Creating an online course can be a time-consuming process, and you will need to be able to work through setbacks and challenges along the way.

You don't need to be an expert in all of these skills, but having a general understanding of them would be beneficial. There are also many resources available that can help you to improve and develop your skills.

If you don't have teachig skills, you can always learn the teaching skills along the way. And if you feel like you need help with the technical side, you can hire a professional to help you with the video production and technical aspects.

Time

The amount of time required to get started with creating an online video course on Udemy can vary depending on several factors. Here are some things to consider:

•   *The complexity of the subject*: The more complex the subject, the more time it will take to research and create the course materials.

• *Your familiarity with the subject*: If you are already an expert in the subject, it will take less time to create the course than if you are new to the subject and need to do extensive research.

• *The length of the course*: The longer the course, the more time it will take to create.

• *The level of production*: The more professional the course needs to be, the more time it will take to record, edit, and produce the videos.

• *Your current skills*: If you are already familiar with video production, marketing, and promotion, it will take less time to create the course than if you are new to these areas and need to learn them first.

On average, it can take anywhere from a few weeks to several months to create a basic course. But it could take even longer if you are creating a longer and more complex course, or if you need to learn new skills along the way.

Creating a course is not a one-time investment; you will need to spend time updating and maintaining the course as well.

Creating an online video course on Udemy can be a time-consuming process, but with some planning, organization, and persistence, you can get your course up and running in no time.

Research

When researching for an online video course on Udemy, there are several important factors to keep in mind:

1.   *Audience*: Make sure you understand your target audience and what their needs and interests are. This will help you create a course that is relevant and valuable to them.

2.   *Competitors*: Research other courses on the same topic to see what is already available and what gaps in the market you can fill with your course. This can also help you to identify what makes your course unique and how you can stand out from the competition.

3.   *Format*: Consider what format your course should take, whether it should be a series of videos, a mix of videos and written materials, or something else.

4.   *Length*: Determine the appropriate length of your course, taking into account the complexity of the subject and the amount of time your target audience is willing to commit to learning.

5.   *Learning objectives*: Clearly define the learning objectives for your course, so that you can ensure that your course will meet the needs of your students and help them to achieve their goals.

6.   *Resources and materials*: Identify the resources and materials that you will need to create your course, such as video equipment, software, and any additional reading materials.

7.   *Up-to-date information*: Make sure that the information in the course is up-to-date and relevant to the current context.

By keeping these factors in mind during your research, you can create a course that is tailored to your target audience, stands out from the competition, and meets the needs of your students.

Topics

Discovering your topic for an online video course on Udemy can be a challenging task, but there are several ways to approach it:

1.   *Look at your existing skills and expertise*: Think about the skills and knowledge you already have, and consider how you can use them to create a course.

2.   *Identify a gap in the market*: Research existing courses on Udemy and other platforms to identify a gap in the market that you can fill with your course.

3.   *Pay attention to your own interests*: Think about the subjects that you're passionate about, and consider how you can share your enthusiasm with others.

4.   *Think about current trends and demands*: Take a look at the current trends in your industry or field, and consider how you can create a course that addresses them.

5.   *Consider your target audience*: Think about the *needs and interests* of your target audience, and consider how you can create a course that will meet their needs and help them achieve their goals.

6.   *Ask for feedback*: Reach out to your friends, family, and colleagues and ask for their opinion on what topic would be interesting for them to learn about.

7.   *Experiment*: Try to create a course on different topics, it may not be the first topic you chose that will be the most successful or the one you enjoy the most.

Finding the right topic can take some time and experimentation, so don't get discouraged if you don't find the perfect topic right away. Keep experimenting, and you'll find the topic that is the best fit for you.

Title and descriptions

Structuring your title and descriptions for an online video course on Udemy is crucial to attracting potential students and making them want to enroll in your course. Here are some tips to structure your title and descriptions effectively:

1.   *Be specific*: Use specific keywords and phrases that accurately describe the content of your course. Avoid being too general or vague.

2.   *Use action words*: Use action words in your title and descriptions to make them more engaging and appealing.

3.   *Use numbers*: Use numbers in your title and descriptions, such as "10 Tips for Writing Effective Emails" or "5 Secrets to Improving Your Memory." Numbers make the title more specific and can make it more attractive.

4.   *Use testimonials*: Use testimonials from previous students in your descriptions to show the effectiveness of your course and build trust with potential students.

5.   *Keep it short and simple*: Keep your title and descriptions concise and easy to read, and avoid using complex language or jargon that may discourage potential students.

6.   *Highlight the benefits*: Use the title and description to highlight the benefits of taking your course, such as what students will learn, what skills they will acquire, and what results they will achieve.

7.   *Be consistent*: Be consistent with the language and tone used in your title and descriptions throughout your course to maintain a professional and cohesive look.

By structuring your title and descriptions effectively, you can help potential students to understand the value of your course and make them more likely to enroll.

Video length

The ideal length of your videos for an online video course on Udemy can vary depending on several factors such as the complexity of the subject, the format of the course, and the attention span of the target audience. There are some general guidelines that you can follow when determining the length of your videos:

1.   *Keep it concise*: Videos that are too long can be overwhelming and can lose the attention of the students. Try to

keep your videos as concise as possible, while still covering all the necessary information.

2.   *Break it down*: Break down complex subjects into smaller, manageable chunks. This will make the course easier for students to follow and understand.

3.   *Consider the format*: If you're using a mix of video and written materials, the video length can be shorter, as the students will have additional resources to read and understand the subject.

4.   *Test it out*: Test different video lengths and formats with a small group of students to see what works best.

5.   *Keep in mind the attention span*: The average attention span of an adult is around 8 seconds, so it's recommended to keep the videos under 8-12 minutes, as it's considered to be the optimal length for online video content.

6.   *Consistency*: Be consistent with the video length throughout the course, so the students can have an idea of how much time they need to dedicate to each module.

The ideal length of your videos will depend on the subject matter, the format of the course, and the target audience. You need to find a balance between keeping the videos concise and making sure that all the necessary information is covered.

Communicate with your students

Communicating with your students is an important part of creating and delivering an online video course on Udemy. Here are some ways to effectively communicate with your students:

1.   *Use the Udemy messaging system*: Udemy has a built-in messaging system that allows you to communicate directly with your students. This is a great way to answer questions and provide support.

2.   *Use the course discussion forum*: Udemy also has a course discussion forum where students can ask questions and share their thoughts about the course. You can use this forum to respond to questions and engage with your students.

3.   *Send out newsletters*: You can use email marketing tools to send out newsletters to your students to keep them informed about updates, new content, and upcoming events.

4.   *Provide a contact email*: Provide a contact email on your course page, so that students can reach you directly if they have any questions or concerns.

5.   *Use social media*: Utilize social media platforms to communicate with your students and build a community. You can use these platforms to share updates, answer questions, and provide additional resources.

6.   *Create a community*: Encourage students to connect with each other and share their learning experience, this will help to build a supportive community and create a sense of belonging.

7.   *Be responsive*: Make sure to respond to student inquiries in a timely manner, this will help to build trust and make students feel valued.

By effectively communicating with your students, you can provide a better learning experience and create a sense of community that will keep your students engaged and motivated.

Promotion

Promoting your online video course on Udemy is an important step in attracting students and generating revenue. Here are different ways how you can promote your course:

1.   *Utilize Udemy's promotion tools*: Udemy has a variety of promotional tools available to instructors, such as coupon codes, email campaigns, and affiliate marketing. Utilize these tools to reach a larger audience and attract new students.

2.   *Use social media*: Share your course on social media platforms to reach a wider audience. Use hashtags and join relevant groups to target your ideal students.

3.   *Leverage your personal network*: Share your course with friends, family, and professional contacts. You can ask them to share your course with their friends and colleagues as well.

4.   *Partner with influencers*: Partner with influencers in your industry to promote your course to their followers.

5.   *Offer a free preview*: Offer a free preview of your course to give potential students a taste of what they can expect. This can be a great way to generate interest and attract new students.

6.   *Create a landing page*: Create a landing page for your course, with all the information and the value proposition of the course; this will help potential students to understand the benefits of taking your course.

7.   *Optimize for search engines*: Optimize your course title and description using keywords, to make it easier for potential students to find your course when searching for related topics.

8.   *Run ads*: Run ads on platforms such as Facebook, Google, or Udemy itself to reach a wider audience and attract new students.

By promoting your course effectively, you can reach a larger audience and generate more revenue. Remember that promotion is an ongoing effort, and you should keep promoting your course even after it's published.

Platforms

Udemy is not the only platform where you can upload and sell your online video course. There are several other platforms you can consider such as:

1.   **Coursera**: Coursera is a leading online learning platform that offers courses from top universities and organizations. You can apply to become an instructor and create your own course, and earn money by creating and teaching a course.

Coursera offers a few different options for instructors. They have partnerships with universities and organizations, and revenue sharing depends on the agreement with the partner. They also have a self-service program called Coursera for Individuals, where instructors pay a subscription fee to create and sell courses.

2.   **Skillshare**: Skillshare is an online learning community where you can create and teach your own course, and earn money through a subscription-based model.

Skillshare operates on a royalty-based model. Instructors earn money based on the number of minutes watched by premium members of Skillshare. They also have a referral program where you can earn a bonus for every new member you bring in.

3.   **Teachable**: Teachable is a platform that allows you to create, market, and sell your own online courses. With Teachable, you can customize the look and feel of your course website, and have access to a variety of tools to grow your business.

Teachable offers different pricing plans for course creators. The platform offers both a free plan with limited features and paid plans with more advanced features. Teachable charges a transaction fee on their free plan, but the transaction fee is waived on their paid plans.

4.   **Thinkific**: Thinkific is another platform that allows you to create and sell online courses. It provides a range of features including course creation, payment processing, student management, and analytics.

Thinkific also offers various pricing plans for course creators. They have a free plan with basic features and paid plans with additional functionality. Like Teachable, Thinkific charges transaction fees on their free plan, but these fees are waived on their paid plans.

5.   **LinkedIn Learning**: LinkedIn Learning (formerly Lynda.com) is an online learning platform that offers courses on a wide range of subjects, from business and technology to creative skills. You can apply to become an instructor and create your own course, and earn money by creating and teaching a course.

LinkedIn Learning is a subscription-based platform, so users pay a monthly fee for access to all the courses. Instructors are typically contracted or invited by LinkedIn Learning and compensated based on agreements made with the platform.

6.   **Kajabi**: Kajabi is an all-in-one platform for creating and selling online courses, membership sites, and marketing automation. It offers features such as website building, email marketing, and analytics.

Kajabi operates on a monthly subscription pricing model. The pricing plans vary depending on the features and functionality you need for your course. The fees typically cover the use of the platform, hosting for your course content, and access to various marketing and sales tools.

These are some of the most popular platforms, but there are many other platforms out there, each with its own set of features, pricing, and audience. It's a good idea to research and compare the different platforms to find the one that best fits your needs and goals.

While the specific pricing details may change over time, you can visit their websites to get the most up-to-date information on their pricing plans and any additional fees associated with using their platform to post and sell your course.

Conclusion

Creating and selling an online course offers a world of opportunities to share your expertise, generate income, and make a positive impact. By leveraging your expertise and passion, conducting market research, and delivering high-quality content, you can create a compelling course that resonates with your target audience. Engaging with your students, marketing your course effectively, and continuously improving based on feedback are key to building a successful online teaching business. Success requires dedication, adaptability, and a commitment to delivering value to your students. With the right approach and mindset, creating and selling an online course can be a fulfilling and rewarding journey that empowers learners around the globe.

#8

POD Sites

Prints and Profits

Print on Demand (POD) sites allow individuals and businesses to create and sell custom products without holding inventory. It is a good way to make money because it requires low start-up costs and minimal risk. POD sites handle production, fulfillment, and shipping, allowing sellers to focus on creating and promoting their designs. Some popular POD sites include Redbubble, Spri.ng, and Zazzle. To start making money with POD sites, you will need to create an account, upload your designs, and set your profit margin. It's also important to market your products through social media and other channels to drive sales. With the right approach, POD can be a profitable and low-stress way to turn your creative ideas into a business.

Who is this ideal for?

Print on Demand (POD) is ideal for a variety of individuals and businesses, including:

1.   *Graphic designers*: POD sites provide a platform for designers to showcase and sell their designs on a variety of products, such as t-shirts, mugs, and phone cases.

2.   *Entrepreneurs*: POD allows individuals to start their own e-commerce business without the need for large investments in inventory or manufacturing.

3.   *Artists*: POD sites give artists a platform to sell their artwork on a variety of products and reach a larger audience.

4.   *Small businesses*: POD can be a cost-effective way for small businesses to expand their product offerings and reach new customers without the need for large investments in inventory.

5.   *Niche product creators*: POD can be ideal for creators of niche products, such as custom-designed clothing for a specific group, like a fan club or a religious group, or for special event like a birthday or a family reunion.

POD is a good fit for anyone who wants to turn their creative ideas into a business, without the need for large investments or inventory management.

Different POD sites

Here are some examples of popular Print on Demand (POD) sites and what they are good for:

1.   **Redbubble**: This POD site is good for artists, graphic designers, and illustrators looking to sell their designs on a wide range of products, including clothing, home decor, and accessories. Redbubble offers a large selection of products and has a strong community of sellers and buyers.

2.   **Spri.ng**: This POD site is good for those looking to sell custom t-shirts and clothing. Spri.ng offers a wide range of

clothing options and has a user-friendly interface for designing and listing products.

3.   **Zazzle**: This POD site is good for businesses and individuals looking to sell custom products such as clothing, home decor, and accessories. Zazzle has a wide selection of products and offers high-quality printing.

4.   **Spreadshirt**: This POD site is good for those looking to sell custom clothing and accessories. Spreadshirt offers a wide range of products and has a user-friendly interface.

5.   **Society6**: This POD site is good for artists and designers looking to sell their work on a wide range of products, including home decor, accessories, and clothing. Society6 offers a large selection of products and has a strong community of sellers and buyers.

All of these POD sites are known for their wide selection of products, easy-to-use interface, and for handling production, fulfillment, and shipping for the sellers, allowing them to focus on creating and promoting their designs. They also have a good reputation for providing a quality product to their customers and have a large customer base.

Better or worse

Here is a comparison between some popular Print on Demand (POD) sites:

1.   **Redbubble vs Spri.ng**: Redbubble offers a wider range of products including clothing, home decor, and accessories. Spri.ng

specializes in custom t-shirts and clothing. Redbubble has a stronger community of sellers and buyers and offers more features for promoting and selling products. Spri.ng offers a user-friendly interface for designing and listing products.

2.   **Zazzle vs Society6**: Zazzle offers a wider range of products including clothing, home decor, and accessories. Society6 specializes in home decor and accessories. Both sites have a strong reputation for providing high-quality printing. Zazzle has a more extensive customization options for some of their products, Society6 has a more curated selection of products.

3.   **Spreadshirt vs Spri.ng**: Spreadshirt offers a wider range of products including clothing and accessories. Spri.ng specializes in custom t-shirts and clothing. Spreadshirt has more customization options for some of their products. Spri.ng offers a user-friendly interface for designing and listing products.

Each site has its own specific features, profit margin, and target audience, so after you research the different options you will see which one aligns best with your goals and the type of products you want to create and sell. Some POD sites may be more popular in certain regions or with certain types of products, so it's also a good idea to consider your target market when choosing a POD site.

Skillset

There are several skills that can be helpful when using a Print on Demand (POD) site to make money:

1.   *Graphic design*: Creating visually appealing designs that will attract buyers is a key skill when using POD sites.

2.   *Marketing*: Promoting your products effectively is crucial for driving sales. Understanding how to use social media, email marketing, and other channels to reach potential customers can be very beneficial.

3.   *Product research*: Knowing how to research the market and identify trending products can help you create designs that will sell well.

4.   *Branding*: Creating a strong brand can help you establish a loyal customer base and stand out from the competition.

5.   *Customer service*: POD sites handle production and fulfillment, but as a seller you will be responsible for communicating with customers and addressing any issues that arise.

6.   *Business acumen*: Running a small business, even with a POD model, still requires you to have a basic understanding of business operations, including financial management and inventory management.

While it's not necessarily required to have all of these skills, having some of them will help you to be more successful in the POD business. You can learn and improve your skills with time and practice.

The process of getting started

The amount of time it takes to get started with a Print on Demand (POD) site can vary depending on a few factors:

1.   Setting up an account: Creating an account on a POD site typically only takes a few minutes. You will need to sign up with your email and confirm, probably ad some details about you.

2.   Designing and uploading products: This can take anywhere from a few minutes to several hours, depending on the complexity of your designs and the number of products you plan to create.

3.   Marketing and promotion: This can take as little or as much time as you want to invest in it. You can start simple by creating social media accounts and promoting your products there, or you can invest more time and resources in advertising campaigns, email marketing, and other strategies to reach a larger audience.

4.   Fulfillment and customer service: POD sites handle the production and fulfillment of orders, but you will need to be available to communicate with customers and address any issues that may arise.

You can get started with a POD site in a matter of hours, but building a successful business takes time and effort. To start seeing sales, you will need to invest time and effort into creating designs, uploading products, and promoting your brand. As with any business, the more time and effort you put in, the more likely you are to see success.

Niches

Choosing a niche is an important step to success. General stores (stores that don't concentrate on one topic) usually don't retain customers. Example: a customer visits your shop because they like a t-shirt with a cat on it. If your other designs are all different then the customer will most likely not come back. However, if your whole shop is cat themed they would most probably come back more regularly to check out your product and even recommend your shop to friends.

There are a wide variety of niches that can be successful on Print on Demand (POD) sites. Here are a few examples:

1.   *Art and illustration*: Artists and illustrators can sell their designs on a wide range of products, including clothing, home decor, and accessories.

2.   *Graphic design*: Graphic designers can create designs for custom products like t-shirts, mugs, phone cases, and more.

3.   *Pop culture*: There is a big market for merchandise related to popular TV shows, movies, and video games.

4.   *Humor and satire*: Funny or satirical designs can be popular on POD sites, especially when they are related to current events or trending topics.

5.   *Fashion and Streetwear*: POD sites can be a great platform for niche fashion designs and streetwear, where you can target specific groups of customers.

6.   *Personalized products*: Some POD sites allow you to create personalized products like custom clothing, phone cases, or mugs with names, images or special messages.

7.   *Special events merchandise*: POD sites are suitable for creating merchandise for events such as weddings, anniversary, birthday, or family reunion.

8.   *Niche interest*: POD sites can be a great platform for niche interest like fan clubs, hobby clubs, or pets.

This is just a small sample of the niches that can be successful on POD sites. It's important to *research the market* and identify a niche that aligns with your interests and skills. Identifying a niche you're passionate about will help you create designs that stand out and attract customers who are interested in your specific niche.

Design creation

There are several ways to create designs for Print on Demand (POD) sites, depending on your design expertise:

1.   If you are a skilled designer: You can create designs using graphic design software such as Adobe Illustrator or Photoshop. These software allow you to create vector or raster designs that can be easily scaled and printed on a variety of products.

2.   If you have basic design skills: You can use free online design tools such as Canva or Adobe Express to create designs. These tools have pre-made templates and design elements that you

can use to create professional-looking designs without needing advanced design skills.

3.   If you don't have any design skills: You can hire a designer to create designs for you. You can find freelance designers on platforms like Upwork or Fiverr.

4.   Using stock images or free resources: You can use stock images or free resources such as icons or illustrations from sites like Unsplash or Pixabay to create your designs. You can combine these images with text or other design elements to create a unique design. Make sure your read their terms and conditions on how to use their images for your designs.

5.   Using pre-made templates: Some POD sites have built-in design tools that allow you to customize pre-made templates. This is a good option if you don't have any design skills, but still want to create your own designs.

The key to creating successful designs is to find a way that works best for you and your skill set. Keep in mind the target audience and the specific niche you are trying to reach when creating your designs.

Ways to promote your products

There are different ways to promote your Print on Demand (POD) sites, for example:

1.   *Social media*: Create accounts on popular social media platforms like Instagram, Facebook, and Twitter, and use them to

promote your products. Regularly share images and information about your products, and use hashtags to reach a larger audience.

2.   *Influencer marketing*: Partner with social media influencers who have a large following in your niche.

3.   *Email marketing*: Build an email list of potential customers and send them regular updates about new products and promotions.

4.   *Paid advertising*: Use paid advertising on platforms like Google AdWords, Facebook, or Instagram to increase visibility for your products.

5.   *SEO*: Optimize your website or POD shop for search engines, so your products appear higher in search results.

6.   *Blogging*: Create a blog and use it to share information about your products, your brand, and your niche. Read more about it in Book 2: Chapter #29 Start A Blog: *Embarking on Blogging Adventures*.

7.   *Community building*: build a loyal following by engaging with customers and creating a sense of community around your brand.

8.   *Giveaways*: Host giveaways or contests on social media to drive engagement and build excitement around your products.

9.   *Affiliate marketing*: Partner with other businesses or individuals to promote your products to their audience.

10.   *Cross-promotion*: Partner with other POD sellers or small businesses to cross-promote each other's products.

Not all promotion strategies will work for every business, so it's a good idea to test a few different approaches and see which ones are most effective for you. Keep in mind that building a loyal following takes time and effort, so be prepared to invest time and resources into promoting your products.

Note: If you want to know how you can create POD products with no design skills search for my Book "AI for POD: How to Use AI Tools To Create Successful Brand" (*Coming Soon*).

Conclusion

In conclusion, Print on Demand (POD) sites provide an accessible and low-risk opportunity for individuals and businesses to make money by selling custom products. The benefits of using POD sites include low start-up costs, minimal inventory management, and the ability to focus on creating and promoting designs. With a wide range of products available, such as clothing, accessories, and home decor, there are ample opportunities to tap into various niches and target specific audiences. Whether you are a skilled designer or someone with no design experience, there are options available to create appealing designs. Promoting your products through social media, influencer marketing, email campaigns, and other strategies can help drive sales and build a loyal customer base. While success may require time and effort, the potential to turn your creativity into a profitable business makes POD sites an enticing avenue for entrepreneurs, artists, and designers alike.

#9

PLR Products

Unlocking PLR Potential

PLR stands for Private Label Rights. It refers to a type of license in which the holder is granted the right to use and edit pre-existing content, and then republish it as their own. This type of license is commonly used for digital products such as eBooks, articles, and videos.

One way to make money with PLR products is to use the content to create your own information products, such as eBooks or courses, and then sell them on your own website or on platforms like Amazon or Udemy. You can also use PLR content to create blog posts, social media posts, or email newsletters to promote affiliate products or your own products.

Another way to make money with PLR products is to use the content to create a membership site or coaching program, where members pay a monthly or yearly fee for access to exclusive content and support.

Examples of PLR products include eBooks on various topics such as "10 Secrets To Success" and "The Ultimate Guide to Yoga" or a set of articles on "Dog Training."

Marketplaces

There are several marketplaces where you can buy and sell digital PLR products. Some popular options include:

1.   IDPLR (https://www.idplr.com/): IDPLR is one of the largest PLR marketplaces, with a wide range of products including eBooks, articles, videos, and software. They have been in the industry for a long time and offer a good selection of products.

2.   PLR.me (https://www.plr.me/): PLR.me is another popular marketplace for PLR products, with a focus on high-quality content in various niche markets. They have a wide range of products, including eBooks, articles, videos, and graphics.

3.   PLR   Products   (https://www.plrproducts.com/):   This website offers a wide variety of PLR products, including eBooks, articles, videos, and software. They also offer a free membership option that gives you access to a limited selection of products each month.

4.   Master Resell Rights (https://www.masterresellrights.com/): This website offers a wide range of PLR and resells rights products, including eBooks, articles, videos, and software. They also offer a free membership option that gives you access to a limited selection of products each month.

5.   WarriorForum (https://www.warriorforum.com/): This is a forum that is well known in the Internet Marketing and PLR industry, there you can find a lot of PLR sellers and buyers, and it's a great place to look for specific niche PLR products.

There are many other marketplaces for PLR products available online. You should research the reputation and credibility of any marketplace before making a purchase to ensure that you are getting high-quality, legitimate products.

How to make money

Buy PLR

There are several ways to make money with PLR products, some of the most popular include:

1.   Create and sell your own information products: Use PLR content to create your own eBooks, courses, or webinars, and then sell them on your own website or through platforms like Amazon or Udemy.

2.   Create and sell website content: Use PLR content to create blog posts, social media posts, or email newsletters, and then sell access to the content on your own website or through a membership site.

3.   Create and sell coaching programs: Use PLR content to create a coaching program or membership site, where members pay a monthly or yearly fee for access to exclusive content and support.

4.   Create and sell physical products: Use PLR content to create physical products like books, journals, or t-shirts and sell them online or in person.

5.   Use PLR content to build an audience: Use PLR content to create blog posts, social media posts, or email newsletters, and

then use the audience you build to promote affiliate products or your own products.

6.   Use PLR content for your business: Use PLR content to create brochures, flyers, or other marketing materials for your own business.

7.   Create and sell video content: Use PLR video content to create video tutorials, how-to's, or other video content, and then sell access to the videos on your own website or through a membership site.

8.   Resell the PLR products: you can buy PLR products, modify them and resell them as your own; this is a good option if you don't have time to create your own content, but have experience in sales and marketing. Make sure you check the rights for the specific PLR product, as they may differ from product to product.

You will need to research the market and evaluate the competition before starting a business with PLR products.

PLR Membership site

You could also create an exclusive membership website where you can sell your PLR products. Here is an example of a structure of such website:

A membership site is a website that allows members to access exclusive content or services in exchange for a monthly or yearly fee. Here is an example of a structure for a membership site that sells PLR products:

1.   **Home**: The Home page of the site should provide an overview of the membership site, including the types of PLR products available and the benefits of joining. It should also include a *call to action* to encourage visitors to sign up for a free trial or paid membership.

2.   **Membership Plans**: The site should offer different membership plans, such as a basic plan that provides access to a limited selection of PLR products, and a premium plan that provides access to a wider selection of PLR products.

3.   **Product Categories**: The site should have a navigation menu that allows members to browse PLR products by categories, such as eBooks, articles, videos, or software.

4.   **Product Pages**: Each PLR product should have its own page, with a detailed description, a preview of the content, a "Buy" or "Download" button, and a detailed description of the right which come with the purchase of the product.

5.   **Member's Area**: Once a member signs up, they should have access to a member's area where they can download PLR products, access exclusive content, and manage their membership.

6.   **Support**: The site should have a support page where members can find answers to frequently asked questions, or contact customer support for help.

7.   **Blog/News**: A blog or news section where you can post updates about new products, sales, and other relevant information.

8.   **Community/Forum**: A section where members can interact with each other, share ideas, and ask questions.

This is just one example of how a membership site for PLR products could be structured, but you can customize it to your needs and the type of PLR products you are selling.

Create the products yourself

Sell PLR

Another option is to create your own products which you can then sell as PLR products. This can be a good way to make money, as you can generate income from the initial sale of the product, as well as from any future sales of the product by others who purchase the PLR rights.

Creating your own PLR products can be time-consuming and requires a significant investment of time, effort, and resources. As with any business, it is important to research the market and competition to ensure that there is a demand for the products you want to create.

Selling PLR products can be a good way to make money if you have specific expertise or knowledge in a particular niche and you can create high-quality and valuable content. Also, you can leverage your existing content and repurpose it into different formats like eBooks, courses, and webinars to sell as PLR products.

Be aware that creating and selling PLR products is a business, and like any business, it requires a solid plan, marketing, and promotion to be successful. You should be prepared to invest time, effort, and money to create high-quality products, and then promote and sell them effectively.

You should make sure that you are familiar with the legal and ethical considerations of creating and selling PLR products, such as copyright laws and the rights and responsibilities of the PLR license.

Rights and responsibilities of the PLR license

When you purchase a PLR license, you are typically granted certain rights to use and edit pre-existing content, as well as certain responsibilities. These rights and responsibilities can vary depending on the terms of the specific PLR license you purchase, but here are some common elements:

Rights:

1.   The right to use the content: You are generally granted the right to use the content for your own personal or commercial use, such as creating and selling your own information products.

2.   The right to edit the content: You are generally granted the right to edit the content as you see fit, such as adding your own branding, rewriting sections, or combining it with other content.

3.   The right to sell the content: You are generally granted the right to sell the content as your own, such as selling eBooks or courses that you have created using the PLR content.

Responsibilities:

1.   The responsibility to give credit: You may be responsible for giving credit to the original creator or source of the PLR content, as per the terms of the license.

2.   The responsibility to not pass on the PLR rights: You may not be allowed to pass on the PLR rights to others, such as reselling the PLR license.

3.   The responsibility to not claim authorship: You may not be able to claim authorship of the content, as per the terms of the license.

4.   The responsibility to follow copyright laws: You may be responsible for following copyright laws and ensuring that the content is not plagiarized or infringing on the rights of others.

Read and understand the terms of the specific PLR license you purchase to ensure that you are aware of your rights and responsibilities. Different countries may have different laws related to PLR, so it's important to research laws in your jurisdiction.

Skillset to sell

Selling digital PLR products is ideal for entrepreneurs, marketers, and business owners who want to create and sell their own information products, such as eBooks, courses, and webinars. It can also be ideal for content creators and bloggers who want to create and sell website content or membership sites.

In terms of skillset, to be successful in selling digital PLR products, you will need:

• Knowledge of the niche or industry you are creating products for.

• Marketing skills to promote and sell your products effectively.

• Writing skills to be able to edit and repurpose the PLR content.

• Business skills to manage your finances, customer service, and other aspects of running a business.

• Technical skills to set up and manage a website, payment processing, and download delivery.

In addition to these skills, you need to have a good understanding of the legal and ethical considerations of creating and selling PLR products, such as copyright laws and the rights and responsibilities of the PLR license.

You have to have a solid plan and strategy on how to create a market and sell PLR products. This includes researching the market to ensure there's a demand for the products you want to create and creating a plan to promote and sell the products effectively.

You can always learn new skills, and there are resources available to help you acquire them. For example, you can take online courses to learn marketing, writing, or business skills, or hire a virtual assistant or freelancer to handle certain aspects of the business.

Payment processing options

Once you set up a website to sell digital PLR products, there are several payment processing options available to you. Some popular options include:

1. **PayPal**: PayPal is one of the most widely used payment processors, and it's easy to set up and use. It allows you to accept payments from customers in over 200 countries, and it's free to sign up.

2. **Stripe**: Stripe is another popular payment processor that is widely used by online businesses. It's easy to integrate with your website, and it offers a wide range of features, including recurring payments and subscriptions.

3. **Square**: Square is a payment processor that is particularly popular among small businesses. It offers a range of features, including the ability to accept payments online and in person.

4. **2Checkout**: 2Checkout is a popular payment processor that supports a wide range of payment methods and currencies. It also offers fraud prevention tools and recurring billing options.

5. **Authorize.net**: Authorize.net is a payment gateway that allows you to accept credit card payments on your website. It also offers fraud prevention tools and can be integrated with a variety of shopping carts.

These are just a few examples of the many payment processing options available. You have to research and compare the features and fees of different options to find the one that best meets the needs of your business.

When choosing a payment processor, you must consider factors such as the fees, the payment methods supported, the level of security, and the ease of integration with your website. You should also check if the payment processor is compliant with the laws and regulations in your jurisdiction.

Can you sell your product multiple times?

The terms of a PLR license can vary depending on the specific license and the seller, but generally, once a product with PLR rights has been purchased, it can be resold multiple times to different buyers. This is known as "white label" rights or "reselling rights" and it allows the buyer of the PLR product to resell it as their own.

Not all PLR licenses include reselling rights. Some PLR licenses may be for personal use only, and others may have limits on the number of times the product can be sold. So it's a good practice to *check the terms* of the specific PLR license you are considering purchasing or selling.

When selling a PLR product multiple times, make sure that the buyers are aware of the fact that it's a PLR product and it's been sold before and to make sure that you are not making any false claims about the product being original or exclusive.

While it is possible to sell a PLR product multiple times, you have to check the terms of the specific PLR license, be transparent with the buyers, and follow legal and ethical guidelines.

Can people repurpose your product?

If multiple people buy the same PLR product and want to repurpose it, it can be an issue if they all use the same content in similar ways, as it can result in duplicate content being published on the internet. This can be a problem because of:

1.   *Search Engine Optimization* (SEO): When there is a large amount of duplicate content on the internet, search engines like Google may have difficulty determining which version of the content is the original. This can result in a lower search engine ranking for all versions of the content, making it harder for people to find your website or product.

2.   *Branding and Reputation*: When multiple people use the same content in similar ways, it can make it difficult for customers to differentiate between the different products or websites. This can dilute your brand and reputation, making it harder to establish trust and credibility with your customers.

3.   *Legal Issues*: If the PLR content that was used is copyright protected and you do not have a proper license, it can lead to legal issues.

With PLR products, the buyers are granted the right to edit and repurpose the content. Therefore, it's possible to make the content unique by rewriting it, adding your own voice, and customizing it for your audience. You can use the PLR content as a starting point and add more value to it, like creating a course, adding videos, audio, templates, worksheets, etc.

Conclusion

Selling digital PLR products can be a great way to make money as an entrepreneur, marketer, or business owner. It allows you to create and sell your own information products, such as eBooks, courses, and webinars, without having to invest the time and effort required to create the content from scratch.

Keep in mind that creating and selling PLR products is a business, and like any business, it requires a solid plan, marketing, and promotion to be successful. It's important to research the market and competition to ensure that there is a demand for the products you want to create, and to create a plan to promote and sell the products effectively.

It's viable that you are aware of the legal and ethical considerations of creating and selling PLR products, such as copyright laws and the rights and responsibilities of the PLR license. Also to be transparent with buyers about the fact that it's a PLR product and it's been sold before.

Selling digital PLR products can be a great way to make money, but it requires time, effort, and resources to be successful. A profitable business can be achieved through research, planning, and proper execution.

#10

Affiliate Marketing

Earnings Unleashed

Affiliate marketing is a rapidly growing industry that has taken the world of online commerce by storm. Simply put, it's a type of online marketing where businesses or individuals partner with other businesses or individuals to promote their products or services in exchange for a commission. As an affiliate marketer, you promote the products or services of another business to your audience, and you receive a commission on every sale that is made through your unique affiliate link.

The potential of affiliate marketing is enormous, as it provides a great opportunity to earn a passive income online. With the right strategies, affiliate marketing can be a highly lucrative business that allows you to work from anywhere in the world, with no inventory, no shipping, and no customer support. The affiliate marketing industry is expected to grow to over $8 billion by 2024, and there is no better time to get started than now. Whether you're an experienced marketer or just starting out, affiliate marketing can be a great way to earn money online and build a sustainable online business that can provide a steady stream of income for years to come.

Ways to make money with affiliate marketing:

1.   Promote affiliate products through your own website or blog. You can write product reviews, create how-to guides, and share your experiences using the product.

2.   Utilize social media platforms such as Instagram, Facebook, and YouTube to promote affiliate products.

3.   Use email marketing to reach out to your subscribers and promote affiliate products.

4.   Utilize influencer marketing and reach out to influencers in your niche to promote your affiliate products.

5.   Look for affiliate programs that offer recurring commissions. This way, you will earn money every time a customer makes a purchase through your affiliate link.

6.   Join affiliate networks such as Commission Junction, ClickBank, and Amazon Associates to find a wide range of products to promote.

Affiliate marketing takes time and effort to see significant results. It's essential to understand your target audience, choose the right products, and promote them effectively.

Is affiliate marketing for you?

Affiliate marketing can be a great opportunity for a wide range of people including:

1.   *Bloggers and content creators*: If you have a blog or website with a significant amount of traffic, you can monetize your content by promoting affiliate products.

2.   *Social media influencers*: If you have a large following on social media platforms such as Instagram or YouTube, you can leverage your audience to promote affiliate products.

3.   *Email marketers*: If you have a large email list, you can promote affiliate products to your subscribers.

4.   *E-commerce store owners*: If you have an e-commerce store, you can promote affiliate products to your customer base.

5.   *Online entrepreneurs*: If you are looking to start an online business, affiliate marketing can be a great way to generate income without having to create your own products.

6.   *Anyone* who is interested in *making money online*.

Affiliate marketing requires a significant amount of time and effort to build a profitable business. It's not a get-rich-quick scheme but with patience and perseverance, anyone can make a success of it.

Skillset

To be successful in affiliate marketing, you will need a combination of the following skills:

1.   *Marketing and promotion skills*: You will need to know how to effectively promote affiliate products to your target audience.

2.   *Content creation skills*: If you plan to promote affiliate products through your own website or blog, you will need to create high-quality content that engages your audience.

3.   *SEO skills*: You will need to understand how search engines work and how to optimize your website or blog for search engines.

4.   *Analytical skills*: You will need to be able to analyze data and track the performance of your affiliate campaigns.

5.   *Communication skills*: You will need to be able to effectively communicate with your audience and potential customers.

6.   *Patience and perseverance*: Affiliate marketing takes time and effort to be successful. You will need to have patience and make quite a few efforts.

7.   *Knowledge of the niche or industry you are targeting*: It's essential to have a good understanding of the industry or niche you are targeting, to be able to *identify the right products* to promote and to be able to communicate with the audience effectively.

8.   *Technical skills*: If you want to create a website, blog or landing page you will need some technical skills or know how to use some website-building tools.

Affiliate marketing is an ever-changing field, so it's important to stay up-to-date on industry trends and best practices and to continuously improve and adapt your skills.

Time

The amount of time it takes to get started with affiliate marketing can vary depending on a few factors:

1.   *Setting up your website or blog*: If you don't already have a website or blog, you will need to set one up. This can take anywhere from a few hours to a few days, depending on your technical skills and the platform you choose to use.

2.   *Creating content*: If you plan to promote affiliate products through your own website or blog, you will need to create high-quality content. This can take anywhere from a few hours to a few days, depending on the length and complexity of your content.

3.   *Finding and joining affiliate programs*: You will need to research and find affiliate programs that are relevant to your niche or industry. This can take anywhere from a few hours to a few days, depending on how much research you need to do.

4.   *Promoting your affiliate links*: Once you have your website or blog set up and you have joined affiliate programs, you will need to start promoting your affiliate links. This can take anywhere

from a few hours to a few days, depending on the promotion method you choose.

5. *Seeing results*: Seeing results from your affiliate marketing efforts can take time, it can take anywhere from a few weeks to a few months, depending on the niche and the method you choose to promote.

In general, you can expect to invest a significant amount of time and effort, in the beginning, to set up your affiliate marketing business and to see results. But as you gain experience and improve your skills, the process should become more efficient and you will be able to see results faster.

Platforms

Here is a list of platforms where you can join affiliate programs:

1. **Amazon Associates**: One of the largest and most popular affiliate programs, with a wide range of products to promote.

2. **Commission Junction**: A large affiliate network that connects businesses with affiliates. Commission Junction has very big and famous brands. To connect with some of them and to join their affiliate program can require having already a website with traffic or big following. If you are just starting out, the bigger brands won't accept you. You can aim for smaller ones. Once you develop your network you might lend also big brands.

3. **ClickBank**: A popular affiliate network that specializes in digital products such as e-books and software.

4.   **ShareASale**: An affiliate network with a wide range of products and merchants to choose from.

5.   **Rakuten Marketing**: A leading affiliate network with a wide range of products and merchants to choose from.

6.   **Awin**: A global affiliate network that connects businesses with affiliates. Especially designed for people who are starting out and small companies.

7.   **PartnerStack**: An affiliate platform that connects businesses with software and SaaS affiliates.

8.   **Impact Radius**: A global affiliate marketing platform that connects businesses with affiliate partners.

9.   **Skimlinks**: A platform that helps content publishers monetize their website with affiliate links.

10.   **Viglink**: A platform that helps content publishers monetize their website with affiliate links.

These are just a few examples, and there are many other affiliate platforms and networks available. It's essential to research and find the platforms that best suit your niche or industry.

Note:

It is important to inform your audience that you use affiliate links. This is a standard practice in the industry and it is also a requirement of the Federal Trade Commission (FTC) in the United States. The FTC requires that website owners disclose when they receive a commission or other compensation for promoting a product. This is to ensure that consumers are aware that the website owner may have a financial interest in the product they are promoting.

The best way to disclose that you use affiliate links is to have a clear and conspicuous disclosure statement on your website or blog. This statement should be placed in a prominent location, such as the footer of your website, or on your "About" page. It should be written in clear and simple language and should inform your audience that you may receive a commission for any purchases made through affiliate links.

In addition to a disclosure statement, you should also make sure to clearly identify affiliate links as such. This can be done by using a different color or font for affiliate links, or by using a disclaimer or disclosure button on or near affiliate links.

By following these guidelines, you can ensure that your audience is fully informed about your use of affiliate links and that you are in compliance with the FTC regulations.

Example:

Here is an example of a disclosure statement that you could use on your website or blog:

"Disclosure: This website may contain affiliate links. If you make a purchase through one of these links, I may receive a commission at no additional cost to you. I only promote products that I believe in and that I think will be beneficial to my readers. I want to clarify that I have not received any free products, services, or other compensation from these companies in exchange for mentioning them on the site. I solely receive compensation through affiliate commissions."

This statement informs your audience that your website contains affiliate links and that you may receive a commission for any purchases made through these links. It also states that you only promote products that you believe in and that you have not been given any free products or services in exchange for promoting them.

You can also mention that you are in compliance with the laws and regulations in your country. For example, "As per FTC guidelines, I want to be transparent and inform you that certain links, posts, photos, and other content on this website are affiliate links. This means that if you make a purchase through these links, I may earn a small commission, but it does not affect the price you pay for the product. Your support through these affiliate links helps to sustain and grow this website."

Keep in mind that these are just examples, and you can adjust the language to suit your tone, audience, and website. But it should give you an idea of the kind of information that should be included in a disclosure statement.

Feel free to use the statement above for your website and modify it to suit your needs.

Choosing the right product

Choosing the right products to promote as an affiliate marketer is crucial to the success of your campaign. Here are some tips on how to choose the right products to promote:

1.   *Understand your target audience*: Knowing your target audience and their needs, wants, and interests will help you to identify products that they are likely to be interested in.

2.   *Research the market*: Research the market and find out what products are currently popular in your niche or industry. Look at trends, best sellers, and customer reviews to get an idea of what products are in demand.

3.   *Check the product's credibility*: Make sure to promote products from reputable companies and brands with a good reputation. You can check customer reviews and testimonials to get an idea of the product's credibility.

4.   *Look for high-commission products*: Look for products that offer a high commission rate. This will help you to make more money from each sale.

5.   *Look for recurring commission products*: Consider promoting products that offer recurring commissions, such as subscription-based products or memberships. This will help you to earn a steady income from each customer.

6.   *Test the products*: Try the products yourself if possible, it will give you a better understanding of their features, benefits, and any potential drawbacks, and you'll be able to promote them more effectively.

7.   *Look for exclusive offers or bonuses*: Some affiliate programs or merchants offer exclusive discounts or bonuses for their affiliates; this can make your promotion more appealing to the audience.

Commission per product

The commission you can make per product as an affiliate marketer can vary greatly depending on the product and the affiliate program. Here are a few examples of commission rates you might encounter:

1.   *Digital products such as e-books or software*: Commission rates for digital products can range from 50-75% of the sale price.

2.   *Physical products*: Commission rates for physical products can range from 2-10% of the sale price.

3.   *Subscription-based products*: Commission rates for subscription-based products can range from 5-20% of the monthly or yearly subscription fee.

4.   *High-ticket items*: Commission rates for high-ticket items such as luxury goods or expensive equipment can range from 1-5% of the sale price.

5.   *Services*: Commission rates for services such as consulting or coaching can range from 20-50% of the sale price.

These are just examples, and commission rates can vary widely depending on the product and the affiliate program. It's important to research the affiliate programs you are interested in to find out what the commission rate is and if there are any other incentives or bonuses.

Some affiliate programs use tiered commissions, where you earn a higher commission rate as you sell more products. Some also offer a flat rate commission, which is a fixed amount regardless of the sale amount.

Quick money?

Making quick money with affiliate marketing is not guaranteed, and it requires a lot of hard work, dedication, and persistence. Here are some tips that may help you to start earning affiliate commissions faster:

1.   *Choose high-converting products*: Look for products that have a proven track record of high conversion rates. These are products that are in high demand and are more likely to convert into sales.

2.   *Leverage social media*: Social media can be a powerful tool for promoting affiliate products. You can use platforms like Facebook, Instagram, Twitter, or YouTube to reach a wider audience and increase your chances of making sales.

3.   *Use paid advertising*: Paid advertising can help you to reach a targeted audience quickly. Platforms like Google Ads, Facebook Ads, or Instagram Ads can be used to promote affiliate products to your target audience.

4.   *Offer bonuses or incentives*: Offering bonuses or incentives can help to encourage people to buy through your affiliate link. These can include things like free e-books, training courses, or consultations.

5.   *Create high-quality content*: Creating high-quality content can help to establish your authority in your niche or industry. This can include blog posts, videos, reviews, or tutorials that provide value to your audience.

6.   *Build an email list*: Building an email list can help you to stay in touch with your audience and promote affiliate products on

an ongoing basis. You can use email marketing tools like Mailchimp or ConvertKit to build and manage your list.

Affiliate marketing is not a get-rich-quick scheme, and it takes time and effort to build a successful affiliate marketing business. By following these tips and remaining consistent in your efforts, you can increase your chances of making affiliate commissions quickly.

Free promotion

There is a cost-effective way to promote your affiliate products. You can use Instagram and Pinterest accounts, as both platforms are free to use. By leveraging these social media platforms, you can reach a wide audience and showcase your products without incurring any advertising costs. It provides an excellent opportunity to engage with potential customers, create appealing visual content, and drive traffic to your website or online store without breaking your budget. Utilizing these free platforms effectively can result in significant exposure and sales for your products.

Conclusion

Affiliate marketing has become a powerful way for individuals and businesses to earn passive income online. It's a low-risk and cost-effective way to promote products and services to a wide audience and earn a commission for each sale made through your unique affiliate link.

As the affiliate marketing industry continues to grow, more and more businesses are turning to affiliate marketing as a way to increase their reach and sales. This presents a great opportunity for affiliate marketers to partner with these businesses and earn a commission for promoting their products.

Affiliate marketing offers a great opportunity for anyone looking to earn passive income online, whether you're a seasoned marketer or just starting out. With the right strategies and mindset, affiliate marketing can be a rewarding and lucrative business that allows you to work from anywhere in the world and earn a steady stream of income for years to come.

#11

Copywriting

Wordsmith's Gold

Copywriting is the process of writing persuasive content that is designed to influence people to take a specific action, such as making a purchase or signing up for a service. It is a crucial aspect of marketing and advertising, and can be used across various mediums including websites, email, social media, and print advertising.

To start copywriting, it is important to understand the target audience and what message the copy is trying to convey. Researching the industry and competition can also provide valuable insights. A strong understanding of grammar, punctuation, and sentence structure is necessary, as well as the ability to write in a clear and concise manner.

Practice is also important to becoming a good copywriter. Writing in a variety of formats and styles, such as headlines, body copy, and calls to action, can help improve skills and develop a unique voice.

Copywriting can be a very rewarding career, as it allows creative expression while also having a direct impact on a business's success. It is also in high demand as businesses of all sizes continue to rely on effective marketing and advertising to reach and engage their target audience.

Is copywriting for you?

Copywriting is ideal for individuals who have strong writing skills and are interested in marketing and advertising. It is also a good fit for those who enjoy researching and understanding different industries and target audiences.

Some key traits that are commonly associated with successful copywriters include:

•   Strong communication skills, both written and verbal.

•   Creativity and to be open to think outside the box.

•   Attention to detail and a knack for proofreading and editing.

•   The ability to write persuasively and in a way that resonates with the target audience.

•   A very good understanding of sentence structure, grammar, and punctuation.

•   To write in a clear and concise manner.

•   Understanding of SEO and web optimization.

•   Work efficient under tight deadlines.

Copywriting can be a great fit for a variety of people, whether they have a background in writing, marketing, or another field. It's a versatile and rewarding career that allows individuals to use their skills to influence and engage with people, and can be done in a variety of industries.

Skillset

There are several key skills that are needed to be a successful copywriter:

1.   **Writing skills**: Strong writing skills are essential for crafting persuasive and compelling copy. This includes a good understanding of grammar, punctuation, and sentence structure, as well as the ability to write in a clear and concise manner.

2.   **Research skills**: Copywriters often need to research the industry and competition in order to understand the target audience and the message that needs to be conveyed.

3.   **Creativity**: Copywriting often requires coming up with new and innovative ideas to capture the attention of the audience.

4.   **Marketing and Advertising skills**: Knowledge of marketing and advertising concepts and best practices can help a copywriter to create effective campaigns.

5.   **Attention to detail**: Proofreading and editing are essential skills for copywriters to ensure that the final product is error-free and polished.

6.   **Understanding of SEO**: Understanding how to write for search engines is important for creating content that can be easily found by the target audience.

7.   **Time management**: Copywriters often work on multiple projects at the same time, and need to be able to manage their time effectively to meet deadlines.

8.   **Understanding of design elements**: Basic understanding of design elements, such as layout, typography and color theory

can be beneficial for copywriters to produce effective and cohesive visuals and copy.

9.   **Adaptability**: Copywriting is a dynamic field, and copywriters need to be able to adapt to changing trends and technologies.

10.   **Interpersonal skills**: Copywriters often work with other members of a team, and need to have good interpersonal skills to collaborate effectively.

Time

The time required to get started with copywriting can vary depending on your level of experience and the amount of time you are able to dedicate to learning and practicing. Some steps that you can take to get started as a copywriter include:

1.   *Learning the basics*: Familiarize yourself with the basics of copywriting, such as writing for different mediums, understanding the target audience, and researching the industry. This can be done by reading books and articles, taking online courses, or attending workshops.

2.   *Practicing your writing*: The more you write, the better you'll get. Practice writing different types of copy, such as headlines, body copy, and calls to action. You can also try writing copy for different industries and target audiences to broaden your skills.

3.   *Building a portfolio*: As you gain experience and become more comfortable with your writing, start building a portfolio of your work to showcase to potential clients or employers.

4.   *Networking*: Building relationships with other copywriters and professionals in the industry can help you learn more about the field and potentially open up new opportunities.

Building a successful copywriting career takes time, effort and patience. It may take several months or even years to develop the skills and experience necessary to become a successful copywriter. By dedicating time and effort to learning the craft and practicing your skills, you can increase your chances of success.

Successful copywriters and what to learn from them

There are many successful copywriters who have made a name for themselves in the industry. Some examples include:

1.   **David Ogilvy**: Known as the "father of advertising," Ogilvy was a pioneer in the field of copywriting. His book "Ogilvy on Advertising" is considered a classic in the industry and offers valuable insights on crafting persuasive copy.

2.   **Joe Sugarman**: An accomplished copywriter and marketer, Sugarman is known for his ability to create compelling and persuasive copy for a variety of products and industries. His book "Triggers" is a great resource for understanding the psychology of consumer behavior.

3.   **Gary Halbert**: Considered one of the most successful copywriters of all time, Halbert's "The Boron Letters" is a must-

read for anyone interested in copywriting. It provides valuable insights into the craft of writing persuasive copy.

4.   **Robert Collier**: Robert Collier is considered one of the most influential copywriters of the early 20th century; his book "The Robert Collier Letter Book" is a classic guide to writing effective sales letters.

5.   **Dan Kennedy**: A marketing and copywriting expert, Kennedy's "No B.S. Direct Marketing" is a great book for learning about marketing and copywriting.

Learning from these successful copywriters can be done by reading their books, articles or blog post, studying their style, and analyzing their campaigns. You can also attend their seminars, webinars or workshops, or follow them on social media to stay updated on their latest work and insights. By studying their techniques and understanding their approach to crafting persuasive copy, you can gain valuable insights that can help you improve your own writing and increase your chances of success.

Advertising

Advertising plays a key role in copywriting as it is the main medium through which copy is presented to the target audience. Copywriting is an essential component of advertising, as it is responsible for creating the written content that is used in advertising campaigns.

Copywriting is used in various forms of advertising, such as:

•	Print advertising: Newspaper and magazine ads, brochures, and flyers.

•	Online advertising: Google ads, Facebook ads, and banner ads on websites.

•	Television advertising: TV commercials and infomercials.

•	Radio advertising: Radio commercials.

•	Out-of-home advertising: Billboards, transit ads, and other outdoor ads.

A good copywriter will use persuasive language, storytelling, and calls to action to influence the audience to take a specific action, such as making a purchase or signing up for a service.

Copywriting can also be used to optimize the ad for search engines. This is known as search engine optimization (SEO) copywriting. This type of copywriting is used to improve the visibility of a website or ad in search engine results pages (SERPs) by using keywords and phrases that are relevant to the product or service.

Advertising and copywriting go hand in hand; copywriting is the process of creating written content that is used in advertising campaigns to influence the audience to take a specific action. It's important to understand the target audience and tailor the message accordingly, use persuasive language, storytelling, and calls to action and optimize the ad for search engines. This includes researching the industry and competition, as well as identifying the key benefits that the product or service offers.

Learn advertising

Learning advertising can be done through a variety of methods, including:

1.   **Education**: Many universities and colleges offer degree programs in advertising, marketing, or communications. These programs can provide a comprehensive understanding of advertising concepts and best practices.

2.   **Online Courses**: There are various online platforms that offer advertising courses, such as Coursera, Udemy, and LinkedIn Learning. These courses can be taken at your own pace and cover a wide range of topics, from copywriting and design to media planning and analytics.

3.   **Books and articles**: Reading books and articles about advertising can provide a wealth of information about the industry. Some classic books on advertising include "Ogilvy on Advertising" by David Ogilvy, "Contagious: How to Build Word of Mouth in the Digital Age" by Jonah Berger, and "Made to Stick" by Chip Heath and Dan Heath.

4.   **Industry events**: Attending industry events such as advertising festivals, trade shows and conferences can be a great way to learn about the latest trends and techniques in advertising.

5.   **Practical experience**: One of the best ways to learn advertising is to gain practical experience through internships or

entry-level positions in advertising agencies or in-house marketing departments.

Learning advertising can be done through a variety of ways, including education, online courses, books and articles, industry events and gaining practical experience. You have to find the method that works best for you and to continue learning and staying up-to-date with the latest trends and techniques in the industry.

Practice copywriting

Practicing copywriting is essential to developing the skills and experience necessary to become a successful copywriter. Here are some ways to start practicing copywriting:

1.   *Write in different formats*: Practice writing different types of copy, such as headlines, body copy, and calls to action. Try writing for different mediums, such as print ads, email campaigns, and social media posts.

2.   *Write for different industries*: Try writing copy for different industries and target audiences to broaden your skills and understanding of how to tailor the message to different groups of people.

3.   *Analyze existing copy*: Look at advertising campaigns and analyze the copy that was used. Try to understand what made the copy effective or ineffective and how you would approach the same campaign differently.

4.   *Get feedback*: Share your copy with friends, family, or other writers and ask for feedback. You will find useful information about your writing style and areas where you could improve.

5.   *Study great copywriters*: Read the work of successful copywriters and analyze their techniques. Study the structure, tone, and language they use, and try to incorporate some of those elements into your own writing.

6.   *Keep a writing journal*: Keep a journal of your writing process, including your thoughts, ideas and drafts; this can help you to track your progress and identify patterns in your writing.

7.   *Try copywriting challenges*: There are many online resources that offer copywriting challenges. These challenges can help you practice writing in different formats, and on a variety of topics.

8.   *Use different tools and software*: Try different tools and software such as Grammarly, Hemingway Editor or Copy.ai to improve your writing and editing skills.

Practicing copywriting takes time and effort, but it's essential to developing the skills and experience necessary to become a successful copywriter. By writing regularly, analyzing existing copy, getting feedback, and studying successful copywriters, you can improve your skills and increase your chances of success.

Websites where you can sign up as a freelance writer

There are several websites where you can sign up as a freelance copywriter:

1. **Upwork**: Upwork is one of the most popular freelance platforms; it connects freelancers with clients from around the world. It's a great place to find copywriting jobs, as well as jobs in other areas such as content writing, editing, and proofreading.

2. **Fiverr**: Fiverr is a platform that connects clients and freelancers. It's easy to set up a profile and start bidding on copywriting jobs.

3. **ProBlogger**: ProBlogger is a platform especially for bloggers and writers. It has a wide variety of copywriting jobs, as well as jobs in other areas such as content writing, editing, and proofreading.

4. **LinkedIn**: LinkedIn is a professional networking website; it also has a job board where you can find copywriting jobs. It's a good idea to create a profile, connect with other professionals and make your services visible to potential clients.

5. **PeoplePerHour**: PeoplePerHour is another platform that connects freelancers with clients. It's a place where people can find writing-related jobs.

6. **FlexJobs**: FlexJobs is a platform that specializes in remote and flexible jobs, which includes copywriting jobs as well.

These are some examples of the many websites available where you can sign up as a freelance copywriter. It's a good idea to sign up for multiple platforms and actively search for job opportunities. Competition can be high on these platforms, you should have a strong portfolio and to tailor your pitches to the specific job you're applying for.

Websites that specialize specifically in copywriting jobs

There are websites that specialize in copywriting jobs:

1.   **Copywriter Collective** (https://copywritercollective.com/): A platform that connects businesses with professional copywriters, they have a wide range of copywriting jobs available, including web copy, email marketing, and social media.

2.   **Clever Copywriting School** (https://www.clevercopywritingschool.com/): A platform that teaches copywriting skills and connect copywriters with clients, they have a job board where you can find copywriting jobs.

4.   **Copy Hackers** (https://copyhackers.com/): A website that offers copywriting courses and resources, they also have a job board where you can find copywriting jobs.

5.   **Contena** (https://www.contena.co/): Contena is a platform that helps freelancers to find high-paying writing jobs; it's a great place to find copywriting jobs for web, social media, email, and other types of content.

6.   **AWAI** (https://www.awai.com/): American Writers and Artists Inc, is an organization that provides copywriting courses, resources, and job opportunities. It's a great place to find copywriting jobs and also gain knowledge and skills to improve your craft.

7.   **Copyblogger** (https://copyblogger.com/): A website that provides resources and courses for copywriting, they also have a job board where you can find copywriting jobs.

Keep in mind that these are just some examples of the many websites available that specialize in copywriting jobs.

Potential income

The amount of money you can make as a copywriter can vary depending on your level of experience, skills, the type of copywriting you specialize in, and the demand for your services.

As a freelance copywriter, you can set your own rates and negotiate with clients. Some freelance copywriters charge by the hour, while others charge by the project. According to the Bureau of Labor Statistics, the median hourly wage for writers and authors was $24 in May 2020. Some freelance copywriters charge more than this, while others charge less.

As an entry-level copywriter, you can expect to make less than more experienced copywriters, but as you gain experience and build a portfolio of successful campaigns, you can increase your rates.

Many copywriters choose to work as freelancers, this way, they can have more control over their income and work schedule. By building a diverse portfolio, networking, and continuously improving their skills, they can increase their earning potential.

A freelance copywriter can charge by the hour, by the project, or by the word. A copywriter working in-house can have a salary of around $52,000 per year.

Conclusion

Copywriting is a dynamic and influential field that plays a crucial role in marketing and advertising. It involves crafting persuasive and compelling content to engage audiences and prompt specific actions. Whether you're a skilled writer looking to specialize in marketing or someone interested in entering the world of creative communication, copywriting offers a rewarding avenue for self-expression and professional growth.

To succeed in copywriting, you will need to develop strong writing skills, understand target audiences, and continuously learn about marketing strategies and trends. By practicing regularly, studying the work of successful copywriters, and staying adaptable to changes in the industry, you can refine your abilities and establish yourself as an effective copywriter.

Remember that copywriting is a journey that requires patience and dedication. Whether you're freelancing or working in-house, the ability to craft compelling messages will always be in demand, offering opportunities to contribute to businesses' success and make your mark in the world of advertising.

#12

Drop Servicing

Drop Serve for Dollars

Drop servicing is a business model where a person or company offers a service to clients, but instead of providing the service themselves, they outsource it to a third party provider. The provider then "drops" the completed service back to the person or company, who then delivers it to the client. This model allows for a wider range of services to be offered, as the person or company can outsource specialized tasks to experts in that field. It also allows for scalability, as the person or company can take on more clients without having to hire more staff. Drop servicing can be used in various industries such as digital marketing, design, programming, and more.

Services

A drop servicing business can offer a wide range of services depending on the industry they operate in and the skills of the third-party providers they outsource tasks to. Some examples of services that a drop servicing business might offer include:

•   Digital marketing services such as social media management, search engine optimization (SEO), and email marketing

• Graphic design services such as logo design, brochure design, and website design

• Web development services such as website building, e-commerce development, and mobile app development

• Writing and editing services such as content creation, copywriting, and proofreading

• Virtual assistance services such as scheduling appointments, making travel arrangements, and data entry

• Customer service support

• Translation services

• Consulting services such as business, financial, legal, and technical consulting.

There are many other services that a drop servicing business can offer depending on the providers that they have access to.

The process of getting started

Starting a drop servicing business can be a relatively simple process, but it will require some planning and preparation. Here are some steps to get you started:

1.   **Identify the services you want to offer**: The first step is to identify the services that you want to offer to your clients. Choose services that align with your skills, interests, and experience, and that you know there is a demand for.

Here are some things to consider when choosing the services you want to offer:

• *Your expertise and experience*: Choose services that you have experience in, and that you feel confident in delivering to clients.

• *Market demand*: Research the market to find out what services are in demand. You can do this by looking at what similar businesses in your area or industry are offering, and by talking to potential clients to find out what their needs and preferences are.

• *Your target market*: Identify your target market, and make sure that the services you choose align with their needs and preferences.

• *Your competition*: Look at what services your competitors are offering, and think about how you can differentiate your services to stand out in the market.

The scalability of the services you want to offer, meaning that the service is easy to outsource and can be delivered by a third-party provider without much supervision from you.

By taking the time to carefully choose the services you want to offer, you can ensure that your business is built on a solid foundation, and that you are well-positioned to meet the needs of your clients and grow your business over time.

2. **Research the market**: Research the market to find out what other businesses in your area or industry are offering similar services. Identify your target market and see what are their needs

and preferences. This research will help you choose want to offer and your pricing strategy.

While researching the market, you can:

• *Identify your target market*: Who are the people or businesses that will be most interested in the services you want to offer? What are their demographics, interests, and needs?

• *Understand your competitors*: Who are the other businesses in your area or industry that offer similar services? What are their strengths and weaknesses? How do they market themselves?

• *Analyze market trends*: Look at the overall trends in your industry. Are there certain services that are becoming more popular? Are there certain technologies or platforms that are becoming more important in your industry?

• *Evaluate the demand for your services*: Identify the demand for the services you want to offer. Are there enough people or businesses that need these services to support your business?

This research should be done on a regular basis, as the market is dynamic and it's important to stay updated on changes in order to adjust your strategy accordingly.

3. **Find third-party providers**: Once you have a clear idea of the services you want to offer, you can start looking for third-party providers to outsource tasks to. You can find providers through online platforms, social media, or networking events. The providers will be responsible for delivering the services to your

clients, so you have to choose providers that are skilled, reliable, and that you feel comfortable working with.

Here are some things to consider when finding third-party providers:

• *Skills and experience*: Look for providers that have the skills and experience necessary to deliver the services you want to offer.

• *Reliability*: Choose providers that you can rely on to deliver services on time and to your clients' satisfaction.

• *Communication*: Look for providers that you can communicate easily with and that you feel comfortable working with.

• *Price*: Consider the prices that the providers charge for the services you need and make sure they align with your own pricing structure.

Finding the right providers may take some time; thoroughly vet the providers before working with them. It's also important to establish clear guidelines and expectations, so the provider knows what is expected from them and how to deliver their services to your clients' satisfaction.

4. **Establish your brand**: Create a brand name, logo, and a website that reflects your business and the services you offer. Make sure that your website is user-friendly and easy to navigate. Your brand is what sets you apart from your competition and creates a connection with your target market. Establishing a strong

brand can help you to build trust with your clients and to attract new ones.

Here are some things to consider when establishing your brand:

• *Brand name*: Choose a brand name that is memorable and easy to pronounce.

• *Logo*: Create a logo that represents your business and the services you offer.

• *Website*: Develop a website that reflects your brand, and that is user-friendly and easy to navigate.

• *Tone of voice*: Develop a tone of voice that reflects your brand and that you will use in all of your communications.

• *Branding guidelines*: Create a set of branding guidelines that define the colors, fonts, and imagery you will use in all of your communications.

Your brand should be consistent across all your communication channels, from your website to your social media profiles, to your email signatures. A consistent brand will help you to build trust with your clients and to attract new ones.

A website is a crucial element of your brand; it's where potential clients will go to find out more about your services, so make sure it's professional and easy to navigate. Your website should have a clear call to action, such as a contact form or a phone number, to make it easy for potential clients to get in touch.

Having a strong brand will help you to stand out in the market, build trust with your clients, and attract new ones.

5.   **Develop a pricing structure**: Determine how much you will charge for your services, and how you will bill your clients. Your pricing strategy should take into account the costs of running your business, such as the cost of third-party providers, marketing expenses, and overhead. It should also take into account the market rates for similar services and your target market's willingness to pay.

Here are some things to consider when developing a pricing structure:

•   *Cost of goods sold (COGS)*: Determine the cost of the goods and services you will be providing to your clients, including the cost of third-party providers and any materials or equipment needed to deliver the service.

•   *Overhead*: Take into account any fixed costs associated with running your business, such as rent, utilities, and insurance.

•   *Profit margin*: Decide on a profit margin that you want to achieve, and use that to determine your prices.

•   *Market rates*: Research the market to find out the rates charged by other businesses offering similar services, and use that information to inform your pricing.

•   *Target market*: Consider the income and spending habits of your target market, and price your services accordingly.

There are different pricing strategies that you can choose from, such as:

•   **Cost-plus pricing**: This strategy involves adding a markup to your costs to determine your prices.

•   **Value-based pricing**: This strategy involves charging what your services are worth to your clients.

•   **Competitive pricing**: This strategy involves charging the same or similar prices as your competitors.

Your pricing strategy should be flexible and open for adjustments, as market conditions and costs may change over time. Also you have to communicate the value of your services to your clients to justify the prices you charge.

6.   **Promote your business**: Once you have your website up and running, start promoting your business through social media, online ads, and word of mouth.

Here are ways how you can promote your business:

•   *Social media*: Use social media platforms such as Facebook, Instagram, Twitter, and LinkedIn to promote your business. Create a business page and post updates, images, and videos that showcase your services and the value you offer to clients.

•   *Online ads*: Use online advertising platforms such as Google AdWords and Facebook Ads to reach potential clients.

• *Content marketing*: Create valuable content such as blog posts, videos, and infographics that will attract potential clients to your website.

• *Networking*: Attend networking events in your industry and introduce your business to potential clients.

• *Referrals*: Encourage clients that are happy with your services to refer friends and family to your website.

The key to promoting your business is to be consistent and to use multiple channels to reach your target market. It's also important to track the effectiveness of your marketing efforts and to make adjustments as needed.

Marketing and promoting your business takes time and effort, but it's essential for attracting clients and growing your business. It's a good idea to have a marketing plan and to budget for it, as it will be a continuous effort to reach and retain clients.

7. **Communicate and manage your providers**: Communicate clearly with your providers, setting expectations and guidelines for the work you need done. Managing your providers is a key to ensure that you can deliver the services on time and to your clients' satisfaction.

Here are some things to consider when communicating and managing your providers:

• *Set clear guidelines and expectations*: Clearly communicate your expectations and guidelines for the work that needs to be done. This includes the scope of the work, the deadline, and any specific requirements or instructions.

• *Regular communication*: Keep in touch with your providers on a regular basis, to ensure that they understand your needs and to stay informed about the progress of the work.

• *Provide feedback*: Provide regular feedback to your providers, both positive and constructive, to help them improve and deliver better results.

• *Manage deadlines*: Keep track of deadlines and ensure that the work is delivered on time.

• *Manage quality control*: Regularly review and test the work delivered by your providers, to ensure that it meets your standards and those of your clients.

Effective communication and management of your providers will help to ensure that the services you offer to your clients are delivered on time and to their satisfaction, which will help to build trust with your clients and attract new ones.

It's also important to have a process in place for handling disputes or issues that may arise with your providers. Having a clear agreement in place, that covers issues such as payment, deadlines, and quality of work, can help to mitigate problems and resolve disputes quickly.

For all the examples provided, no matter in which country you plan to start your business, it is important that you open a business bank account. This will help you separate your personal and business finances and also will facilitate tracking your business expenses.

8.   **Get your legal and financials in order**: Make sure that your business is properly registered and that you have the necessary licenses and permits. Set up a system for accounting and tax purposes.

Get your legal and financials in order: Starting a business requires compliance with legal and financial requirements, so get your legal and financials in order before you begin.

Examples for different countries:

USA

Here are some things to consider when getting your legal and financials in order if your business is in the USA:

•   *Register your business*: Register your business with the appropriate government agency, such as the Secretary of State or the Internal Revenue Service (IRS).

https://spaceland.quora.com/What-are-the-most-favourable-days-to-start-a-business-in-2023 (Author's name. Title of Document. Title of Website. Sponsor of Website. Date of Document. Date of Access. URL.)

•   *Obtain necessary licenses and permits*: Make sure you have all the necessary licenses and permits to operate your business in your area.

- *Establish an accounting system*: Set up an accounting system to track your income and expenses, and to prepare financial statements.

- *Get an Employer Identification Number* (EIN): Obtain an EIN from the IRS, which is used to identify your business for tax purposes.

- *Get business insurance*: Consider getting business insurance to protect your business from potential risks.

Laws and regulations can vary by state, country and industry, so you can consult with a lawyer, accountant, or other professional to ensure compliance with all the legal and financial requirements.

Failure to comply with legal and financial requirements can result in fines, penalties, and legal action, so take the time to get your legal and financials in order before you begin. Keep your legal and financials up to date and to seek the advice of professionals as needed.

Starting a drop servicing business can take some time and effort, but with the right planning and preparation, you can build a successful business that offers a wide range of services to clients.

UK

Here are some specific things to consider when getting your legal and financials in order if your business is in the UK:

•   *Register your business*: Register your business with Companies House, which is the government agency responsible for registering companies in the UK.

•   *Choose a business structure*: Decide on the business structure that best suits your business, such as a sole trader, partnership, or limited company.

•   *Obtain necessary licenses and permits*: Make sure you have all the necessary licenses and permits to operate your business in your area. This can vary depending on the type of business you are running and the location.

•   *Establish an accounting system*: Set up an accounting system to track your income and expenses, and to prepare financial statements. You must keep records and submit annual accounts to Companies House, and file a self-assessment tax return to HM Revenue and Customs (HMRC) if you are self-employed.

•   *Register for VAT*: If your business's turnover exceeds the VAT threshold, you must register for VAT and charge VAT on goods and services you provide.

•   *Get Employer's Liability Insurance*: By law, if you have any employees, you must have employer's liability insurance to protect your business against claims made by employees for work-related injury or illness.

•   *Get other business insurance*: Consider getting other types of business insurance to protect your business from potential risks, such as public liability insurance and professional indemnity insurance.

Keep in mind that laws and regulations can change over time in the UK, so you must stay informed and to seek the advice of professionals as needed. You can also check the UK government's business website for more information on the legal and financial requirements for starting a business in the UK.

Germany

Here are some specific things to consider when getting your legal and financials in order if your business is in Germany:

• *Register your business*: Register your business with the local trade office (Gewerbeamt) and the tax office (Finanzamt).

• *Choose a business structure*: Decide on the business structure that best suits your business, such as a sole trader, partnership, or limited liability company (GmbH).

• *Obtain necessary licenses and permits*: Make sure you have all the necessary licenses and permits to operate your business in your area, such as a trade license (Gewerbeschein)

• *Establish an accounting system*: Set up an accounting system to track your income and expenses, and to prepare financial statements. You must keep records and submit annual accounts to the tax office and other authorities.

• *Register for VAT*: If your business's turnover exceeds a certain threshold, you must register for VAT and charge VAT on goods and services you provide.

• *Get liability insurance*: Consider getting liability insurance to protect your business from potential risks.

- *Comply with labor laws*: Make sure you comply with German labor laws, which include things like minimum wage, vacation days, and working hours.

You can also check the German Federal Ministry for Economic Affairs and Energy's website for more information on the legal and financial requirements for starting a business in Germany.

France

Here are some specific things to consider when getting your legal and financials in order if your business is in France:

- *Register your business*: Register your business with the local Chamber of Commerce and Industry (CCI) and the tax office (URSSAF or URF).

- *Choose a business structure*: Decide on the business structure that best suits your business, such as an auto-entrepreneur, a simplified joint stock company (SAS) or a limited liability company (SARL).

- *Obtain necessary licenses and permits*: Make sure you have all the necessary licenses and permits to operate your business in your area, such as a trade license (licence d'entreprise)

- *Establish an accounting system*: Set up an accounting system to track your income and expenses, and to prepare financial statements. You must keep records and submit annual accounts to the tax office and other authorities.

• *Register for VAT*: If your business's turnover exceeds a certain threshold, you must register for VAT and charge VAT on goods and services you provide.

• *Get liability insurance*: Consider getting liability insurance to protect your business from potential risks.

• *Comply with labor laws*: Make sure you comply with French labor laws, which include things like minimum wage, vacation days, and working hours.

You can also check the French government's business website for more information on the legal and financial requirements for starting a business in France.

Starting a business is always different depending on the country you live in, so make sure you make an extensive research about the laws in your country.

Licenses and permits

To find out more about the necessary licenses and permits for your business in a specific location, you can take the following steps:

1.   Contact your local Chamber of Commerce or Industry: Your local Chamber of Commerce or Industry can provide you with information on the licenses and permits required for your business and how to obtain them.

2.   Check with your local government website: Many local government websites have information on the licenses and permits required for different types of businesses and how to obtain them.

3.   Consult with a lawyer or accountant: A lawyer or accountant familiar with the laws and regulations of your specific location can provide you with guidance on the licenses and permits required for your business.

4.   Research industry-specific requirements: If your business operates in a specific industry, research the industry-specific requirements and regulations that apply to your business.

5.   Get in touch with an industry association: Joining an industry association can be a great way to get information on the licenses and permits required for your business, they can inform you of any changes to laws and regulations.

The requirements for licenses and permits can vary by location and by industry, so research the specific requirements for your business and consult with professionals as needed.

Establishing an accounting system

1.   *Determine your accounting needs*: The first step in setting up an accounting system is to determine the specific needs of your business. This includes identifying what financial information you need to track, such as income, expenses, and taxes, as well as any specific reporting requirements you may have.

2.   *Choose accounting software*: There are a variety of accounting software options available that can help you track and manage your financial information. Some popular options include QuickBooks, Xero, and Sage. These software options typically offer features such as invoicing, expense tracking, and financial reporting.

3.   *Set up chart of accounts*: Setting up a chart of accounts allows you to organize your financial information and track income and expenses by category. This will help you to easily see where your money is coming from and where it's going.

4.   *Input financial data*: Once you have your chart of accounts set up, you can begin inputting your financial data, such as sales, expenses, and payments.

5.   *Review and reconcile*: Regularly review and reconcile your financial data to ensure accuracy. This includes reconciling your bank account and credit card statements with the transactions recorded in your accounting software.

6.   *Generate reports*: Generate financial reports such as profit and loss statements, balance sheets and cash flow statements, to monitor the financial health of your business and make informed decisions.

7.   *Keep accurate records*: Keep accurate records of all financial transactions and retain receipts, invoices and other documents for at least six years.

8.   *Seek professional help*: As your business grows, it may be beneficial to seek the help of an accountant or bookkeeper to help you manage your accounting and tax compliance.

There are many accounting software options available, both paid and free, that can help you to establish an accounting system. Research the different options and choose the one that best fits the needs of your business.

Techniques to earn money

There are several ways to earn money with a drop servicing business:

1.   *Offer services at a markup*: One way to earn money with a drop servicing business is to offer services at a markup. This means that you charge your clients more than what it costs you to outsource the service to a third-party provider. The difference between the cost and the price you charge is your profit.

2.   *Offer recurring services*: Another way to earn money is to offer recurring services, such as monthly website maintenance or social media management. This can create a stream of revenue for you and your business.

3.   *Upsell additional services*: Once you have established a relationship with a client, you can upsell additional services, such as website design or graphic design.

4.   *Bundle services*: Offer bundle services, by combining several services into one package, you can increase the value of your offering and charge more for it.

5.   *Affiliate marketing*: Partner with other businesses and earn a commission for referring clients to them.

6.   *Offer consulting services*: You can also earn money by offering consulting services to help your clients improve their online presence and grow their business.

7.   *Charge a retainer*: Charge a retainer fee for your services, this is a recurring fee paid by your clients for your services.

To increase your revenue, you need to constantly identify new opportunities and ways to improve your services, this will help you to attract and retain clients, which will help your business grow.

Conclusion

Starting a drop servicing business can be a great way to earn money while working from home. By outsourcing certain tasks to third-party providers, you can offer a wide range of services to your clients without having to handle all the work yourself.

Starting a drop servicing business does require some planning and effort. You will need to research and identify the services you want to offer, find reliable providers, set up a pricing structure, and promote your business to attract clients.

By following the steps outlined in this guide, you can set up a solid foundation for your drop servicing business and position yourself for success. By being diligent, persistent and flexible, you can grow your drop servicing business and achieve financial success.

#13

Becoming A Captioner

Earnings in Words

Captioning is the process of creating written descriptions of audio or visual content to make it accessible for people who are deaf or hard of hearing. It can also provide a transcript of the audio for people who are non-native speakers or who prefer to read the dialogue. Becoming a captioner requires a strong grasp of the English language, as well as knowledge of captioning software and techniques. It is typically done on a freelance or contract basis, and pay can vary depending on the company or organization hiring the captioner. Potential earnings can range from $25,000 to $75,000 per year. As the need for accessibility services increases, the demand for captioners is likely to grow.

The process of getting started

To get started as a captioner, you will need to have a strong command of the English language, as well as knowledge of captioning software and techniques. Here is how you could start your career:

1.   *Get the necessary education or training*: Look for captioning or transcription courses offered by community colleges, vocational schools, or online. Some captioning companies may also provide on-the-job training.

2.	*Build your skills*: Practice captioning different types of videos and audio files, such as news broadcasts, TV shows, and movies. This will help you develop your skills and become more comfortable with the captioning process.

3.	*Get certified*: Some organizations, such as the National Court Reporters Association, offer certification programs for captioners. This can help you stand out to potential employers and show that you have the necessary skills and knowledge for the job.

4.	*Look for job opportunities*: There are a variety of companies and organizations that hire captioners, including television and media companies, educational institutions, and government agencies. You can also look for freelance or contract work on job boards and online platforms.

5.	*Keep yourself updated*: As technology and accessibility standards are changing rapidly, it is important to keep yourself updated with the latest software and best practices.

Software and techniques

There are a variety of captioning software and techniques that a captioner should be familiar with. Some of the most popular include:

1.	*Automatic speech recognition (ASR) software*: This type of software uses artificial intelligence to transcribe spoken words into written text. Examples include Speechmatics, Otter.ai, and Google Speech-to-Text.

2.   *Professional captioning software*: These software allow you to create captions manually by typing or syncing the text with the audio. Examples include Aegisub, FAB Subtitler, and CaptionMaker.

3.   *Real-time captioning*: This technique involves captioning live events, such as news broadcasts, court proceedings, and webinars. It requires specialized software and equipment, and is typically done by trained stenographers.

4.   *Pre-recorded captioning*: This technique involves captioning pre-recorded videos or audio files. It can be done manually or with software, and requires knowledge of syncing the captions with the audio.

5.   *Subtitling*: This is the process of adding text to a video in order to provide a translation of the dialogue for non-native speakers. It's similar to captioning but the text is usually smaller, and not necessary to have the non-speech information in the video.

Captioning is a regulated field and there are standards that captioners should follow, such as the FCC closed captioning standards in the USA, so it's important to stay updated with these regulations as well.

Software costs

The cost of captioning software can vary depending on the type of software and the provider. Some software is available for free, while others require a subscription or a one-time purchase. Here's a general idea of what you can expect to pay for different types of captioning software:

1.   Automatic speech recognition (ASR) software: Some ASR software is available for free, while others require a subscription. Prices can range from $0 to $200 per month.

2.   Professional captioning software: Prices can vary widely depending on the software. Some software is available for free, while others can cost up to several thousands of dollars.

3.   Real-time captioning equipment: Real-time captioning equipment is typically more expensive than other captioning software. A stenography machine can cost anywhere from $4,000 to $7,000, and a software can cost from $1,000 to $2,000.

4.   Subscription-based online platforms: Some online platforms offer a subscription-based model where you pay monthly or annually to use their service. Prices can range from $20 to $100 per month.

        Some of the software have a free trial option, where you can try the software for a certain period of time before purchasing it, this could be a good way to test the software and see if it fits your needs before committing to a purchase.

Websites for captioning jobs

        There are several websites where you can find captioning jobs. Here are a few popular options:

1.   **Upwork**: This is a freelance job platform that connects freelancers with clients who need their services. You can create a profile and apply for captioning jobs posted by clients.

2.   **Rev**: This is a captioning and transcription company that hires freelancers to caption and transcribe audio and video files.

3.   **3Play Media**: This is a company that provides captioning, transcription, and audio description services to businesses, universities, and government agencies. They hire freelance captioners to work on their projects.

4.   **GoTranscript**: This is a company that provides transcription and captioning services to clients around the world. They hire freelancers to caption and transcribe audio and video files.

5.   **Crowdsurf**: This is a platform that connects freelancers with clients who need captioning and transcription services.

6.   **Indeed**: This is a job search engine that allows you to search for captioning jobs across a wide range of industries and companies.

7.   **LinkedIn**: This is a professional networking site that allows you to search for captioning jobs and connect with potential employers.

8.   **CaptioningStar**: This is a transcription and captioning company that provides services to clients in the media, entertainment, and education industries. They hire freelance captioners to work on their projects.

9.   **Vanan Captioning**: This is a company that provides captioning services to clients in the entertainment, education, and corporate industries. They hire freelance captioners to work on their projects.

10.   **VITAC**: This is a company that provides captioning, transcription, and audio description services to clients in the media and entertainment industries. They hire freelance captioners to work on their projects.

All of the above companies offer work as a freelancer, and typically you can apply for the job via their website and go through a screening process before getting hired. Some of them may also have tests to evaluate your skills and knowledge of the field before assigning the job to you.

These are not the only websites available and there are other platforms, companies and agencies that may offer captioning jobs, so it's recommended to do some research and try to find what may fit better for you.

Conclusion

Becoming a captioner is a great career choice for those with a strong command of the English language (or any other language) and an interest in making audio and visual content more accessible for people who are deaf or hard of hearing. It's a field that is in demand and with the growing awareness of accessibility and inclusion, it's expected to continue to grow in the future. To get started as a captioner, you will need to have the necessary education or training, practice captioning different types of videos and audio files, and stay updated with the latest software and best practices. There are many job opportunities available, from freelance and contract work to full-time positions with companies and organizations. With the right skills, dedication and a bit of luck, you can make a successful career as a captioner.

#14

Building Apps

App Architecture

Building apps can be a great way to make money, whether you have coding knowledge or not. There are several ways to create apps without coding, such as using a drag-and-drop app builder or hiring a developer to create the app for you. If you do have coding knowledge, you can create and publish your own apps on app stores such as the Apple App Store and Google Play Store. Monetization methods include in-app purchases, paid downloads, and advertising. You can also build apps and sell them to other businesses or individuals. Whatever your approach, do thorough market research to ensure that there's a demand for your app and to find the right monetization strategy.

Is building apps for you?

Building apps can be a great opportunity for a variety of people, depending on the approach they take.

If you don't have any coding knowledge, using a drag-and-drop app builder can be a good option. This approach is ideal for entrepreneurs, small business owners, or anyone who has an idea for an app but doesn't have the technical skills to create it themselves.

If you have coding knowledge, building and publishing your own apps on app stores can be a great way to make money. This approach is ideal for developers, programmers, and anyone with the skills to create their own apps.

If you have an idea for an app but don't want to do the development work, you can hire a developer to create the app for you and then monetize it. This is ideal for entrepreneurs, small business owners, or anyone with a great app idea but without the technical skills to create it.

Building and selling apps to other businesses or individuals can be a great way to make money. This approach is ideal for developers, programmers and anyone with the skills to create apps and market it to the right audience.

Building apps can be a great opportunity for anyone with a great idea and the drive to turn it into a successful business.

Skillset

The skills needed to build apps will vary depending on the approach you take.

If you're using a drag-and-drop app builder, the main skill you'll need is the ability to navigate and use the app builder's interface. You may also need some basic design skills to create the look and feel of your app.

If you're building and publishing your own apps on app stores, you'll need strong coding skills in the programming languages used to build the app. For example, iOS apps are typically built with SwiftUI or Objective-C, while Android apps are built with Java or Kotlin. You'll need a good understanding of app design and user experience, as well as a solid understanding of the app store guidelines.

If you're hiring a developer to create your app, you'll need to have a good understanding of what you want the app to do, as well as the ability to communicate your ideas clearly to the developer. You'll need to have a good understanding of the app store guidelines and be able to market your app effectively.

If you're building and selling apps to other businesses or individuals, you'll need to have strong coding skills, as well as a good understanding of the business needs of your clients. You'll need to have good communication and marketing skills to be able to sell your apps effectively.

Overall, building apps requires a combination of technical skills, design skills, and business acumen.

Drag-and-drop app builders

There are several popular drag-and-drop app builders that can be used to create apps without coding, including:

•   Appy Pie: Appy Pie is a popular app builder that allows users to create apps for iOS, Android, and Windows platforms. It has a simple and easy-to-use interface and offers a wide range of features including push notifications, in-app purchases, and integration with social media platforms. The prices start from 12$/month.

• BuildFire: BuildFire is another popular app builder that allows users to create apps for iOS and Android. It offers a wide range of features such as push notifications, in-app purchases, and integration with popular services such as Zendesk. BuildFire also has a plugin store where you can add more features to your app. One of its advantages is that it has a wide range of customization options, but also has its limitations, like having to pay for some of the features.

• GoodBarber: GoodBarber is a platform that allows users to create apps for iOS and Android. It offers a wide range of features including push notifications, in-app purchases, and integration with social media platforms. One of its advantages is that it's easy to use and it has a wide range of design options. It also has its limitations, such as being more expensive than other app builders.

These are a few examples of popular drag-and-drop app builders, and note that each platform has its own advantages and disadvantages. Research and compare different options to find the one that best suits your needs and goals.

Research

When conducting market research for an app, pay attention to the following:

1.   **Target market**: Understand who your app is intended for and what their needs and wants are. Research their demographics, location, and behavior patterns.

2.   **Competitors**: Identify existing apps in your app's niche, and analyze their strengths and weaknesses. Look for opportunities to improve upon what's already available and to differentiate your app from the competition.

3.   **Market size and growth**: Research the size of the market for your app and the potential for growth. Identify trends and patterns in the market to understand the future potential of your app.

4.   **Revenue models**: Understand the different revenue models available for your app and which one is the most suitable for your app and target market.

5.   **User feedback**: Ask your target market for feedback on your app idea and consider their suggestions and concerns.

6.   **App store ranking**: Understand how app store ranking algorithms work and how to optimize your app's visibility on app stores.

7.   **Advertising**: Identify the best channels to advertise your app and how to reach your target audience effectively

8.   **Cost**: Understand how much it will cost to develop, market and maintain your app, and if the projected revenue will be able to cover the costs.

By paying attention to these key factors, you can gain a deeper understanding of the market for your app and identify opportunities for success.

App monetization

There are several ways to monetize an app, including:

1. *In-app purchases*: Offer users the ability to purchase additional features, content, or virtual goods within the app.

2. *Paid downloads*: Charge users a one-time fee to download the app from the app store.

3. *Subscriptions*: Offer users a monthly or annual subscription for access to premium content or features.

4. *Advertising*: Include ads in the app and earn revenue based on the number of views or clicks.

5. *Sponsorships*: Partner with businesses to feature their products or services in the app in exchange for a fee.

6. *Freemium Model*: Offer the app for free but charge for additional features or remove ads.

7. *In-app referrals*: Reward users for referring new users to download the app.

8. *White-labeling*: Sell the app to other businesses or individuals who can then brand it as their own.

9. *API access*: Allow other businesses or developers to access your app's functionality through an API in exchange for a fee.

Different monetization methods may be more suitable for different types of apps and target markets. Thoroughly research and test different monetization strategies to find the one that works best for your app.

Monetizing your app through API access.

Here's a more detailed explanation of how this can be done:

API stands for Application Programming Interface, and it's a set of protocols, routines, and tools for building software and applications. By creating an API for your app, you can allow other businesses or developers to access the functionality of your app and use it in their own projects.

To execute this monetization strategy, you would need to develop an API for your app that can be accessed by external parties. This can be done by using a framework or platform that allows you to create and manage APIs, such as Express.js, Flask, or Ruby on Rails.

Once your API is ready, you would need to market it to potential customers and set a pricing plan for access to the API. You can charge a flat fee, a monthly subscription, or a pay-per-use model.

This strategy may require a significant investment in terms of development time and resources, but it can provide a sustainable source of revenue for your app. It's important to have a clear and comprehensive documentation and support for the API, and also make sure that it complies with the regulations and policies of the market you are targeting.

Creating an API for your app can be a powerful way to monetize your app by providing value to other businesses and developers, but requires a clear plan and execution.

Sell your app as white label app

There are websites where you can sell your app as a white-label solution. White labeling is the practice of selling a product or service under a different brand and it allows other businesses to use your app as their own.

Here are a few examples of websites where you can sell your white-label app:

1. Chupamobile: Chupamobile is a marketplace for buying and selling ready-made mobile apps. They offer a wide range of white-label apps for different platforms including iOS and Android, and you can sell your app on their platform.
2. SellMyApp: SellMyApp is a marketplace where people can buy and sell mobile app source codes. You can sell your app source code as a white-label solution on their platform, and they will help you market it to potential buyers.
3. CodeCanyon: CodeCanyon is a marketplace for buying and selling scripts and code. You can sell your app source code as a white-label solution on their platform and they help with the promotion and showcasing of your app.
4. UpWork and Freelancer: platforms where you can find potential buyers for your white-label app, you can create a portfolio and showcase your app, and then connect with businesses and entrepreneurs looking for white-label apps.

While these websites can be a great way to market your white-label app, you should still conduct your own research and outreach to potential buyers to maximize your chances of success.

Conclusion

Selling white-label apps can be a lucrative opportunity for app developers and entrepreneurs. Websites like Chupamobile, SellMyApp, CodeCanyon, and platforms like UpWork and Freelancer provide avenues to market and sell your white-label apps. It's essential to carefully consider the advantages and disadvantages of each platform.

These platforms offer exposure to a wide audience and often provide marketing and promotional services, which can increase the visibility of your app. They also offer a range of apps for different platforms, allowing potential buyers to find suitable solutions. The high level of competition among sellers on these platforms can make it challenging to stand out, and commission fees may impact your profit margin.

It's crucial to conduct thorough research, consider the specific requirements of your app, and evaluate which platform aligns best with your goals. Exploring other avenues for marketing and selling your app, such as networking and self-promotion, can really pay off at the end of the day.

Leveraging white-label app marketplaces and platforms can be a valuable strategy to monetize your app and reach a broader customer base. By understanding the advantages and disadvantages of each platform, you can make informed decisions and increase your chances of success in the competitive app market.

#15

Become A Research Assistant

Assisting Online

Becoming a research assistant is an excellent way to gain hands-on experience in a specific field of study and contribute to the advancement of knowledge in that area. Research assistants typically work under the supervision of a professor or senior researcher, and are responsible for a variety of tasks including data collection, analysis, and manuscript preparation. This type of work can be both challenging and rewarding, as research assistants have the opportunity to learn new skills, work with cutting-edge technology, and contribute to the scientific community. A research assistant typically requires a strong academic background, excellent research and analytical skills, and the ability to work independently and as part of a team. This can be a fulfilling career path for students and recent graduates looking to gain experience in a particular field, or for those interested in pursuing a career in research.

Skillset

To become a research assistant, it is important to have a strong academic background in the field of study related to the research project. In addition, research assistants should have the following skills:

1.   *Strong research and analytical skills*: Research assistants should be able to conduct literature reviews, analyze data, and draw conclusions based on their findings.

2.   *Attention to detail*: Research assistants must be able to work with precision and accuracy in order to ensure that data is collected and analyzed correctly.

3.   *Time management*: Research assistants often work on multiple projects simultaneously, and need to be able to manage their time effectively in order to meet deadlines.

4.   *Communication and writing skills*: Research assistants need to be able to communicate effectively with their supervisors and other team members, as well as write up their findings in a clear and concise manner.

5.   *Technical skills*: Depending on the specific field of research, research assistants may need to have knowledge of specific software or equipment.

6.   *Flexibility and adaptability*: Research projects can be unpredictable and may require research assistants to adapt to changing circumstances.

7.   *Teamwork*: Research is often a collaborative process; research assistants must be able to work effectively as part of a team.

8.   *Strong ethical principles*: Research assistants must be aware of ethical considerations related to research and adhere to them.

Research assistants may also have to be proficient in a foreign language if the research they are conducting is in a different language; it depends on the specific project they are working on.

The process for getting started

Here are some steps to get started as a research assistant:

1.   *Develop your academic background*: To become a research assistant, it is important to have a strong academic background in the field of study related to the research project. Consider pursuing a degree or taking courses in a field that interests you.

2.   *Build your skillset*: Develop the skills that are important for research assistants, such as research and analytical skills, attention to detail, time management, and communication and writing skills.

3.   *Look for opportunities*: Research assistant positions are often advertised on university websites, job boards, and professional networking sites. You can also reach out to professors or researchers in your field of interest and inquire about any available opportunities.

4.   *Apply for positions*: When you find a position that interests you, make sure to submit a well-written and polished application. Tailor your resume and cover letter to the specific position and highlight your relevant skills and experience.

5.   *Prepare for an interview*: If you are selected for an interview, be prepared to discuss your qualifications, experience,

and interest in the research project. Research the project and the organization and come prepared with questions to ask.

6.   *Get involved*: Once you land the position, make sure to ask questions, and be proactive in your work. Showing initiative and a willingness to learn can help you move up in the ranks.

7.   *Network*: Building connections with other researchers and professors in your field can help you find future job opportunities or even be helpful for your own research.

8.   *Consider pursuing a graduate degree*: A graduate degree can be helpful for many research-related careers and many research assistantships are for graduate students.

Getting started as a research assistant can be competitive, so you need to be persistent and not to get discouraged if you don't get your first opportunity.

Platforms

There are several platforms where you can apply for research assistant positions:

1.   *University websites*: Many universities have job boards or career centers that list available research assistant positions. Check the websites of universities in your area or in the field of study you're interested in.

2.   *Professional networking sites*: LinkedIn, and other professional networking sites can be great resources for finding research assistant positions. You can also use these sites to connect with researchers and professors in your field.

3.   *Job boards*: There are many job boards that list research assistant positions, such as Indeed, Monster, and Glassdoor. You can search for positions by location, field of study, or keyword.

4.   *Professional associations*: Many professional associations have job boards or career centers that list research assistant positions. Check the websites of associations related to your field of study.

5.   *Government agencies*: Some government agencies offer research assistant positions. These positions can be found by searching for opportunities on the agency's website or by searching for opportunities through a job search website.

6.   *Non-profit organizations*: Some non-profit organizations conduct research and may offer research assistant positions. Check the websites of organizations in your field of interest.

Remember that getting a research assistant position can be competitive, make sure to tailor your application to the specific position and project and always have a good resume and cover letter ready. Networking and building connections can also be very helpful in finding a research assistant position.

AskWonder

AskWonder is a research service that provides businesses and individuals with on-demand access to a team of researchers who can help answer a wide range of questions. Researchers on the platform can help businesses and individuals quickly find information on a variety of topics, such as market research, industry trends, and competitor analysis.

As for the jobs, AskWonder hires researchers to work on a freelance basis. They are typically looking for researchers who have experience in one or more specific fields and are able to conduct research and provide information quickly and accurately. Researchers are able to set their own schedule and work from anywhere, as long as they have an internet connection.

The platform is looking for researchers with skills in a variety of areas such as:

- Market research

- Industry trends

- Competitor analysis

- Data analysis

- Business analysis

- Financial analysis

- Writing and editing

- Content creation

- Data collection

- Information gathering

AskWonder also hires researchers with experience in specific industries such as technology, healthcare, finance, and more. If you're interested in working as a researcher on the platform, you can apply by submitting your resume and a cover letter on the company's website. They will review your application and if they think you'd be a good fit, they will get back to you.

Other platforms

There are several other sites similar to AskWonder where people can find research jobs:

1.   **Upwork**: Upwork is a popular platform that connects freelancers with clients looking for a wide range of services, including research. You can create a profile, set your rate, and apply for research jobs in various fields.

2.   **Fiverr**: Fiverr is another platform that connects freelancers with clients looking for a wide range of services, including research.

3.   **Freelancer.com**: Freelancer.com is another platform that connects freelancers with clients looking for a wide range of services, including research.

4.   **Indeed**: Indeed is a job search website where you can find a variety of research-related jobs, including research assistant, market research, and data analyst positions.

5.   **Glassdoor**: Glassdoor is a job search website where you can find a variety of research-related jobs, including research assistant, market research, and data analyst positions.

6.   **LinkedIn**: LinkedIn is a professional networking site where you can find a variety of research-related jobs, including research assistant, market research, and data analyst positions.

7.   **Researchpool**: Researchpool is a platform that connects independent researchers with investors, asset managers, and other financial professionals. Researchers can work on a freelance basis and apply to different projects.

8.   **ResearchGATE**: ResearchGATE is a professional network for researchers and scientists. Researchers can use the platform to network and find job opportunities.

These platforms are not exclusively focused on research job and you might find some other jobs that aren't research related, but overall they are good places to start looking for research related jobs.

Conclusion

Becoming a research assistant is an excellent way to gain hands-on experience in a specific field of study and contribute to the advancement of knowledge in that area. Research assistants typically work under the supervision of a professor or senior researcher, and are responsible for a variety of tasks including data collection, analysis, and manuscript preparation. To become a research assistant, it is important to have a strong academic background in the field of study related to the research project, as well as a set of skills such as research and analytical skills, attention to detail, time management, and communication and writing skills.

There are many platforms where you can find and apply for research assistant positions, such as university websites, professional networking sites, job boards, professional associations, government agencies, and non-profit organizations. AskWonder is one such platform that provides businesses and individuals with on-demand access to a team of researchers who can help answer a wide range of questions.

Keep in mind that getting a research assistant position can be difficult, make sure to tailor your application to the specific position and project and always have a good resume and cover letter ready. Networking and building connections can also be very helpful in finding a research assistant position. And remember that this is a great opportunity to gain experience, learn new skills and grow in a specific field of study; it could be a very fulfilling and rewarding career path.

#16

CPA Marketing

Navigating Online Ads

CPA (Cost Per Action) marketing is a form of online advertising in which a business pays a commission to an affiliate for each specific action taken by a user as a result of clicking on an affiliate's promotional link. The action can be anything from a sale, lead, or even a simple form submission. CPA marketing is considered to be a more cost-effective form of online advertising as it only requires payment when a specific action is taken, rather than paying for clicks or impressions. CPA marketing allows for more precise targeting of potential customers as businesses only pay for the actions that are most likely to lead to a conversion.

Is CPA marketing for you?

CPA marketing can be a good way for affiliates or publishers to make money by promoting a business's products or services and earning a commission for each specific action taken by a user as a result of clicking on their promotional link. It can be particularly beneficial for those who have a large audience or a strong presence in a specific niche, as they can effectively target and promote offers to their audience. CPA marketing can be a good option for those who are experienced in online marketing and understand how to drive targeted traffic to offers. Success in CPA marketing requires a significant amount of traffic and a high conversion rate, so it may not be the best option for those who are new to online marketing or have a small audience.

Skillset

To be successful in CPA marketing, there are several skills that are important to have:

1.   *Understanding of online marketing*: CPA marketing is an online-based form of advertising, so you will need a good understanding of the various channels and tactics that can be used to drive targeted traffic to offers.

2.   *Knowledge of target audience*: In order to effectively promote offers, it's important to have a good understanding of the target audience and be able to identify and target those who are most likely to take a specific action.

3.   *Analytical skills*: CPA marketing requires constant monitoring and optimization to ensure that campaigns are performing well and that the cost per action is within a profitable range.

4.   *Creativity*: Success in CPA marketing often requires coming up with new and creative ways to promote offers to a target audience.

5.   *Technical skills*: Understanding of web design and basic HTML, CSS, and JavaScript can be helpful in creating landing pages, setting up tracking and conversion pixels and troubleshoot technical issues that may arise.

6.   *Patience*: It may take time to build up a significant amount of traffic and see a return on investment in CPA marketing, so patience is important.

7.   *Flexibility*: The CPA industry is constantly changing, and new trends and offers will appear, so being able to adapt to new strategies and opportunities is important to keep earning money with CPA.

While these skills can be helpful, they can also be acquired and developed over time with practice and learning.

Time

The amount of time needed to get started with CPA marketing can vary depending on a number of factors, such as the level of experience you have with online marketing, the size of your audience, and the specific offers you are promoting.

If you are new to online marketing and CPA, it may take some time to learn the basics and understand how to effectively drive targeted traffic to offers. Building up a significant amount of traffic can take time, and it may take some experimentation to find the right offers and strategies that work for your audience.

With some time and effort, it is possible to get started with CPA marketing relatively quickly. Many CPA networks have a signup process that only takes a few minutes, and once you are approved, you can start promoting offers right away.

CPA marketing is not a get rich quick scheme and it takes time and effort to see results, but with patience and persistence, you can start seeing results in a reasonable amount of time.

CPA Networks

Here is a list of some popular CPA networks where you can sign up to start promoting offers:

1.   MaxBounty   https://www.maxbounty.com/

2.   ClickDealer   https://www.clickdealer.com/

3.   Commission Junction https://www.cj.com/

4.   CPAlead   https://www.cpalead.com/

5.   CPAGrip   https://www.cpagrip.com/

6.   OfferVault   https://offervault.com/

7.   PartnerStack

        https://partnerstack.com/partners-and-publishers

8.   affmine   https://affmine.com/

9.   OGAds   https://ogads.com/

Not all CPA networks are open for new members, some have strict rules and verification processes before accepting new affiliates, also some of them are specific to certain countries, and some may specialize in certain types of offers or niches. Therefore it's a good idea to research and compare multiple networks before joining one.

Finding the best offer

Finding the best CPA offer for you can be a bit of a trial-and-error process, but there are some strategies that can help you identify the best offers for your audience. Here are a few tips to help you find the best CPA offer for you:

1.   *Understand your audience*: The best offers for you will be the ones that are most relevant to your audience. Therefore, you will need a good understanding of your target audience and the types of products or services that they are most likely to be interested in.

2.   *Research different offers*: Look for offers from multiple CPA networks and compare them based on factors such as payout, conversion rate, and the overall quality of the offer.

3.   *Check for the landing page's quality*: the landing page is the page where the user will land after clicking on the offer; make sure that the page is well-designed and optimized to convert users.

4.   *Look for offers with high payouts*: Higher payouts may indicate that the offer is more likely to convert and generate a higher return on investment.

5.   *Test and optimize*: Once you have found a few offers that you think would be a good fit for your audience, test them to see which ones perform the best. Use the data you gather to optimize your campaigns and improve your return on investment.

6.   *Look for exclusive offers*: Some CPA networks offer exclusive offers that are only available to selected affiliates, these offers tend to have higher payouts and conversion rates.

7.   *Niche specific offers*: If you have a specific niche, look for offers that are tailored to that niche, for example, if you have a health blog, look for health-related offers.

By following these tips, you should be able to find the best CPA offers for your audience and improve your chances of generating a high return on investment.

Application process

Many CPA networks have an application process that you must go through before you are approved to promote offers. The application process can vary from network to network, but typically it involves filling out an application form and providing some basic information about yourself and your online marketing experience. Some networks may also require you to provide a website or social media account to verify your online presence.

The approval process can take some time and not all applications are accepted, some networks are more selective than others. Some networks may also require you to meet certain qualifications or have a certain level of experience before you can be approved. Some networks may also require you to submit additional information or go through a phone interview as part of the application process.

How to Make Money with CPA Marketing

In CPA marketing, you can make money by promoting CPA offers and earning a commission for each specific action taken by a user as a result of your promotion. Here's an example to illustrate how you can make money with CPA marketing:

Let's say you join a CPA network and find an offer for a free trial of a health supplement. The offer pays $30 per successful trial sign-up.

You create a promotional campaign: You might create a blog post or a landing page that informs your audience about the benefits of the health supplement and includes a call-to-action to sign up for the free trial.

You drive targeted traffic: Using various online marketing channels like social media, search engine optimization, or paid advertising, you direct relevant and interested users to your promotional content.

Users click on your affiliate link: When users click on your affiliate link within your content, they are directed to the offer's landing page.

Users complete the desired action: If the user signs up for the free trial by submitting their information, it is considered a successful action or conversion.

You earn a commission: For each successful trial sign-up generated through your affiliate link, you earn a commission of $30.

The more targeted traffic you drive to your offer and the higher the conversion rate, the more commissions you can earn. By scaling your promotional efforts and optimizing your campaigns, you can increase your earnings in CPA marketing.

The specific commission rates, offers, and conversion actions can vary widely in CPA marketing, and it's crucial to choose offers and strategies that align with your audience and marketing capabilities.

Conclusion

CPA marketing remains a dynamic field that presents both opportunities and challenges. Successful affiliates and publishers understand their audience, employ creative marketing techniques, and leverage data analytics. CPA networks have evolved to attract top affiliates and ensure reliable reporting. Looking ahead, staying adaptable to industry trends, and upholding ethical practices will be crucial. In this ever-changing landscape, CPA marketing will continue to hold the potential for both, profitability and growth.

#17

Niche Websites

Sites for Success

Creating niche websites refers to building a website that focuses on a specific topic or market segment, often referred to as a "niche." This can be done by creating content and resources around a specific topic, such as a hobby, industry, or lifestyle, and building an audience of people interested in that topic.

By focusing on a specific niche, you can build a more targeted and engaged audience, which can make it easier to monetize the website through advertising, affiliate marketing, sponsored content, and other methods. Having a niche website can also help with search engine optimization, as the website can rank better for specific keywords related to the niche.

Creating niche websites also means targeting specific keywords, for which you can optimize your site for SEO and provide relevant content for the visitors.

Finding a profitable niche and creating a successful website in that niche takes time and research. It's a good idea to validate the niche before investing time and resources in it.

Is this for you?

Creating niche websites can be ideal for a variety of people, including:

1.   Entrepreneurs and small business owners looking to expand their online presence and reach a specific audience.

2.   Content creators and bloggers who are passionate about a specific topic and want to build an audience around that topic.

3.   Affiliate marketers who want to promote specific products or services to a targeted audience.

4.   Digital marketer who wants to target specific keywords and get more organic traffic to the website.

5.   Anyone with expertise or knowledge in a particular field who wants to share that information with others and potentially monetize their expertise.

Creating niche websites is not for everyone. It requires time, effort, and commitment to research and create content around a specific topic. It's important to have a solid understanding of online marketing and website creation in order to build a successful niche website.

Skillset

To create niche websites, you will likely need a combination of the following skills:

1. *Content creation*: The ability to write engaging and informative content that appeals to your target audience.

2. *Search Engine Optimization (SEO)*: Knowledge of how to optimize your website and content for search engines in order to increase organic traffic.

3. *Web design and development*: Knowledge of how to design and build a website, including familiarity with website building tools and platforms.

4. *Marketing and promotion*: Knowledge of how to promote your website and build an audience, including through social media, email marketing, and other online marketing techniques.

5. *Niche research*: Ability to research and identify profitable niches with potential for growth and audience engagement.

6. *Monetization*: Knowledge of how to monetize a website through various methods such as advertising, affiliate marketing, sponsored content, and selling products or services.

7. *Analytics and metrics*: Knowledge of how to track and analyze website traffic and user behavior in order to optimize your website and marketing efforts.

While having all of these skills would be ideal, it's not necessary to have them all in order to create a niche website. You can always learn as you go and outsource some tasks if needed.

Examples of CMS

A CMS, or Content Management System, is a software application that allows users to easily manage, create, and publish digital content. Some examples of popular CMS include:

1.   **WordPress**: WordPress is an open-source CMS that is widely used for creating websites of all types, from blogs to e-commerce sites. It is easy to use and customize, making it a popular choice for beginners and professionals alike.

2.   **Joomla**: Joomla is another open-source CMS that is widely used for creating websites. It is known for its extensibility and scalability and is often used for creating larger and more complex websites.

3.   **Drupal**: Drupal is an open-source CMS that is known for its flexibility and powerful features. It is often used for creating websites for organizations and businesses that require advanced functionality.

4.   **Shopify**: Shopify is a popular e-commerce platform that allows users to easily create and manage online stores. It includes features such as inventory management, order processing, and payment integration.

5.   **Wix**: Wix is a website builder that allows users to easily create and manage websites without any coding knowledge. It is a popular choice for small businesses and individuals who want to create a website quickly and easily.

6.   **Squarespace**: Squarespace is a website builder that allows users to create and manage websites with a drag and drop interface.

It's known for its sleek and modern design and it's often used for portfolios and online stores.

These are just a few examples of the many different CMS options available.

Time

The amount of time required to get started with creating a niche website can vary depending on several factors, such as your experience with website creation and online marketing, the complexity of your website, and the niche you have chosen.

If you are new to website creation and are using a website builder or a CMS like WordPress, it can take some time to familiarize yourself with the platform and learn how to use it effectively. With some dedication and effort, you should be able to create a basic website within a few days to a week.

If you want to create a more complex website, or if you are using a more advanced CMS like Drupal, it may take several weeks or even months to get the website up and running.

Once the website is built, keep in mind that creating quality content and building an audience takes time. It's not uncommon for it to take several months or even years to build a sizable audience and monetize the website.

Creating a niche website requires ongoing effort and maintenance, including updating content, monitoring analytics, and improving the website's performance and user experience.

The amount of time required to get started with creating a niche website can vary, but with dedication and effort, you should be able to get a basic website up and running within a few days to a week and start building an audience over time.

Find a profitable niche

Finding a profitable niche for your website can take some research and effort, but here are a few steps that can help:

1.   *Research your interests and passions*: Look for topics that you are passionate about and have a good understanding of, as this will make it easier to create content and build an audience.

2.   *Identify a specific niche*: Once you have identified a broad topic, narrow it down to a specific niche. For example, instead of "fitness", focus on "vegan bodybuilding" or "postpartum fitness".

3.   *Research the competition*: Look at other websites in your niche and see what they are doing well and what they are not. Identify any gaps in the market that you can fill with your website.

4.   *Check the demand*: Look for keywords related to your niche and see how many searches they get per month. Use tools like Google Keyword Planner to check the search volume and competition of your keywords.

5.   *Analyze the profit potential*: Look for ways to monetize your website, such as through advertising, affiliate marketing, sponsored posts, and e-commerce. Estimate the potential revenue you could earn from these methods.

6.   *Validate your niche*: Once you have identified a niche, validate it by talking to people in the niche, researching the audience demographics and looking for customer pain points.

7.   *Test your niche*: Create a landing page or a blog post and drive some traffic to it, to see if people are interested in the topic and if they convert into leads or sales.

Finding a profitable niche takes time and effort, and it's important to validate the niche before investing time and resources into creating a website. Even if the niche seems profitable, you will need to have a unique angle or approach to stand out in the market.

Creating content

Creating content for your niche website can be an ongoing process, but here are a few steps that can help:

1.   *Identify your target audience*: Understand who your target audience is and what their needs, interests, and pain points are.

2.   *Research your niche*: Stay up-to-date on the latest trends, news, and developments in your niche. This will help you create relevant and engaging content that addresses the current needs of your audience.

3.   *Plan your content*: Use an editorial calendar to plan out your content in advance.

4.   *Create valuable content*: Focus on creating content that provides value to your audience. This can include informative articles, how-to guides, tutorials, reviews, and more.

5.	*Use different types of content*: Mix up the types of content you create to keep things interesting for your audience.

6.	*Optimize your content for SEO*: Optimize your content for search engines by including relevant keywords, meta tags, and internal links.

7.	*Promote your content*: Share your content on social media, email, and other channels to promote it and attract more readers.

8.	*Engage with your audience*: Encourage readers to leave comments and feedback on your content and respond to their questions and comments. This will help build a sense of community and engagement around your website.

Creating content for your niche website requires time, effort and dedication. Always think about your target audience and their needs, and focus on providing value to them with your content.

Keywords

Finding keywords for your niche website can help you optimize your content for search engines and attract more organic traffic to your website. Here are a few steps you can take to find keywords for your niche:

1.	*Brainstorm keywords*: Start by brainstorming a list of keywords that are related to your niche. Think about the topics and questions that your target audience might be searching for.

2.	*Use keyword research tools*: Use keyword research tools like Google Keyword Planner, SEMrush, Ahrefs, or others to find additional keywords related to your niche. These tools can also show you data such as search volume, competition and CPC (cost per click) of the keywords.

3.	*Analyze your competition*: Look at other websites in your niche and see what keywords they are targeting. You can use tools like SEMrush, Ahrefs or Majestic to find which keywords your competitors are ranking for.

4.	*Look for long-tail keywords*: Long-tail keywords are more specific and longer phrases that are less competitive and can help you attract more targeted traffic.

5.	*Optimize your content*: Once you have a list of keywords, optimize your content by including them in your headlines, subheadings, and body text. Don't stuff your content with keywords, make sure it reads naturally.

The number of keywords you need depends on the size of your website and the amount of content you plan to create. A general rule of thumb is to target around 1-2 main keywords per page and a few secondary keywords. Remember that targeting too many keywords can actually hurt your website's search engine performance.

Keyword research is an ongoing process, and you will need to keep track of your website's performance and adjust your keyword strategy as needed.

Monetization

Here are some ways of how to monetize your website:

1.   *Advertising*: You can sell advertising space on your website to businesses looking to reach your audience. This can include banner ads, sponsored posts, and native advertising.

2.   *Affiliate marketing*: Promote products or services and earn a commission for them. This can include promoting products through affiliate links, sponsored reviews, or affiliate programs. Check chapter #10 "Affiliate Marketing: *Earnings Unleashed"* for more information (page147).

3.   *Sponsored content*: You can work with brands to create sponsored blog posts, videos, or other content that feature their products or services.

4.   *Selling products*: If you have a product or service of your own, you can sell it through your website. This can be physical or digital products or different services such as consulting or coaching.

5.   *Paid memberships or subscriptions*: If you have valuable content or a community that people are willing to pay for, you can charge for access to your website.

6.   *E-commerce*: If you have a niche that can be monetized through e-commerce, you can start an online store and sell products directly to your audience.

7.   *Sponsorships*: If you have a large audience or a strong social media presence, you can partner with businesses to create sponsored content or promote their products.

Monetizing a website often takes time and effort, and it can be helpful to have a solid audience and a well-defined niche before trying to monetize your website. Also, you can diversify the ways of monetizing and not to rely on one single source of income.

Not all methods of monetization will be appropriate for every website, and you have to find out the methods that best fit your audience and niche.

Conclusion

In conclusion, creating a niche website can be a rewarding endeavor that allows you to share your passion, expertise, and knowledge with a targeted audience. Monetizing your niche website requires careful planning and execution, as well as a deep understanding of your audience's needs and preferences.

By providing valuable content, optimizing for search engines, and engaging with your audience, you can attract traffic and build a loyal following. From there, you can explore various monetization strategies such as advertising, affiliate marketing, sponsored content, selling products or services, memberships, and sponsorships.

Building a successful niche website takes time, effort, and ongoing dedication. It may require continuous research, content creation, and marketing to stay relevant and competitive. It's also crucial to adapt and evolve your monetization strategies based on your audience's feedback and changing market trends.

The success of your niche website will depend on the quality of your content, your ability to connect with your audience, and your persistence in refining your monetization strategies. With the right approach and a focus on providing value, your niche website can become a valuable platform for both your audience and yourself.

#18

Teach A Language

Online Earnings

Teaching a language is the process of helping learners acquire the skills necessary to understand, speak, read, and write a new language. This can be done through a variety of methods, such as classroom instruction, online courses, and self-study materials. Effective language teaching requires a thorough understanding of the language being taught, as well as an understanding of the needs and learning styles of the learners. It also requires the use of appropriate teaching methods and materials, and the ability to provide feedback and support to learners as they progress. Whether teaching a second language to students in a school setting or helping adult learners acquire a new language for professional or personal reasons, the goal is to help learners achieve fluency and proficiency in the language.

Skillset

To become a tutor and teach a language, there are several skills that are important to have:

1.   *Fluency in the language being taught*: A tutor should have a high level of proficiency in the language they are teaching, including a strong command of grammar, vocabulary, and idiomatic expressions.

2.   *Pedagogical skills*: A tutor should have knowledge of language teaching methodology and be able to adapt their teaching style to the needs and learning styles of their students.

3.   *Cultural knowledge*: A tutor should have an understanding of the culture and customs of the people who speak the language they are teaching, as this can help learners better understand and use the language.

4.   *Patience and flexibility*: Tutoring can be challenging, and a tutor must be able to adapt to the needs of their students and be patient when working through difficult concepts or material.

5.   *Good communication skills*: A tutor should be able to effectively communicate with their students and provide clear, concise explanations and instructions.

6.   *Technology skills*: In today's digital age, having the ability to use technology such as online learning platforms, virtual meeting tools, and other digital resources can be an added advantage.

7.   *Adaptability*: Being able to adapt to the student's learning style, level, and individual needs is important.

8.   *Organizational skills*: A tutor should be able to plan, organize, and manage their time and resources effectively.

Platforms and Requirements

There are several platforms available for individuals interested in becoming a tutor, including:

1.   *Online tutoring marketplaces*: These platforms connect tutors with students who are seeking language instruction. Some popular examples include iTalki, Verbling, and Preply. Requirements for becoming a tutor on these platforms typically include fluency in the language being taught, a computer with a stable internet connection, and a webcam. The application process usually involves creating a profile, completing an application form, and providing proof of qualifications and experience.

2.   *Private tutoring*: Many language tutors work independently, and offer private language instruction to individuals or small groups. Requirements for becoming a private tutor include fluency in the language being taught, and a degree or certification in language teaching or a related field. The application process typically involves creating a website or online profile, and reaching out to potential clients through social media, online classifieds, or word-of-mouth.

3.   *Language schools*: Some language schools hire language tutors to teach classes in-person or online. Requirements for becoming a tutor at a language school typically include fluency in the language being taught, and a degree or certification in language teaching or a related field. The application process usually involves submitting a resume, cover letter, and possibly an interview.

The requirements and application process may vary depending on the platform or organization you are applying to, so it's best to check their website or contact them directly for more information.

Earning potential

The amount a language tutor can earn can vary widely depending on a number of factors, including the type of platform or organization they are working with, their qualifications and experience, the language they are teaching, and the location and cost of living.

1.   *Online tutoring marketplaces*: Tutors on online tutoring marketplaces can earn anywhere from $10 to $50 per hour or more, depending on their qualifications and experience. Some tutors charge higher rates for specialized instruction, such as exam preparation or business language instruction.

2.   *Private tutoring*: Private tutors can set their own rates, and can earn anywhere from $20 to $100 per hour or more, depending on their qualifications and experience, and the location and cost of living.

3.   *Language schools*: Tutors working for a language school typically earn a salary, which can range from around $30,000 to $60,000 or more per year, depending on the location and cost of living, and the level of experience and qualifications.

The earning potential for language tutors can vary widely, and the above figures should be taken as rough estimates. Other factors like the location and time of the teaching, the number of hours worked, and the number of students taught can also affect the earning potential of a language tutor.

Conclusion

Becoming a language teacher can be a rewarding and profitable career choice. With the increasing demand for language education both in-person and online, the job market for language teachers is growing. The ability to speak more than one language is a highly sought-after skill, and the demand for language education is on the rise.

Being a language teacher provides an opportunity to share your passion for language and culture with others. It also allows you to develop your own skills and expertise in the language you are teaching. Working as a language teacher also offers a flexible schedule, which can be beneficial for those who have other responsibilities.

The earning potential for language teachers is also quite good. As mentioned earlier, the earning potential can vary widely depending on factors such as platform, qualifications, experience, location and cost of living. The earning potential is generally good and the earning can be high if you are able to establish yourself as a reputable and experienced language teacher.

Becoming a language teacher can be a fulfilling and profitable career choice. With the increasing demand for language education, the opportunity to share your passion for language and culture with others, and the good earning potential, it is definitely worth considering. With the right qualifications and experience, you can become an effective and successful language teacher.

#19

Viral Website

Sites That Soar

A viral website is a website that becomes popular through a viral process of Internet sharing, typically through video, social media, and blogs. To make money with a viral website, you can use a variety of monetization methods such as advertising, affiliate marketing, sponsored content, and selling products or services. You can also consider growing your website and expanding into other businesses such as e-commerce, lead generation, and consulting. Creating a viral website and monetizing it can be a challenging endeavor. In a saturated online landscape, it's crucial to develop a clear strategy and establish a unique value proposition to distinguish yourself from the competition. By offering something distinctive and compelling to your target audience, you increase your chances of creating a website that captures attention, generates significant traffic, and ultimately yields revenue. Remember, it takes careful planning, innovation, and perseverance to succeed in the dynamic world of viral websites.

Is this for you?

Creating a viral website can be a suitable option for individuals or businesses that are looking to establish a strong online presence, increase brand awareness and drive traffic to their website. It can be especially beneficial for content creators, influencers, and entrepreneurs in the entertainment, lifestyle, and tech industries. If you are in a niche market and you can create a website that becomes the go-to source for that niche, it can be a valuable source of income for you.

Creating a viral website requires a significant amount of time, effort, and resources. It's not something that can be achieved overnight, and it requires a clear strategy, consistent content creation, and a strong understanding of the target audience.

Skillset

To create a viral website, you will need a combination of technical and creative skills, some of which are:

1.   *Content creation*: The ability to create high-quality, engaging, and shareable content that resonates with your target audience.

2.   *SEO (Search Engine Optimization)*: The ability to optimize your website and content to rank well in search engines, making it more visible to potential visitors.

3.   *Social media marketing*: The ability to effectively promote your website and content on social media platforms and grow your following.

4.   *Web design and development*: The ability to create a visually appealing and user-friendly website that is optimized for conversions.

5.   *Analytics*: The ability to track and analyze website traffic and engagement metrics to identify opportunities for improvement and measure the effectiveness of your efforts.

6.   *Marketing*: The ability to understand your target audience and create a marketing strategy that appeals to them and drives them to your website.

7.   *Flexibility*: The ability to be flexible and adapt your strategy based on the data, analytics, and user behavior.

Creating and maintaining this type of website is a long-term effort and you may need to have a team with diverse skill sets to achieve it.

Time

The amount of time required to get started with creating a viral website can vary depending on a number of factors, such as the complexity of your website, the size of your team, and your overall strategy. Here are some things to have in mind:

1.   *Content creation*: If you're starting from scratch, it can take some time to create a backlog of high-quality content to populate your website.

2.   *Web design and development*: Depending on the complexity of your website, it could take several weeks or months to design and develop it.

3.   *SEO*: Optimizing your website for search engines can also take time, as it requires research, keyword analysis, and on-page optimization.

4.   *Marketing*: Building a social media following, creating a marketing plan, and promoting your website can also take time.

Creating a viral website is a long-term effort and it may take several months or even years to establish a significant online presence and generate significant traffic to your website. If you have a clear strategy, a consistent effort, and a diversified approach, you can start seeing results and improvement in a relatively short time.

The process of getting started

Here are a few steps you can take to get started with creating a viral website:

1. *Define your target audience*: Understand who your target audience is, what their interests are, and what kind of content they are looking for.

2. *Develop a content strategy*: Create a plan for the type of content you will create how often you will post, and which channels you will use to promote it.

3. *Build your website*: Create a visually appealing and user-friendly website that is optimized for conversions. Make sure it is mobile-friendly and has a responsive design.

4. *Optimize for SEO*: Research keywords, optimize your website's on-page elements, and create high-quality content that is relevant to your target audience.

5. *Promote your website*: Use social media, email marketing, and other marketing channels to promote your website and attract visitors.

6. *Analyze and improve*: Track your website's performance using analytics tools such as Google Analytics, and use the data to identify areas for improvement and optimize your strategy accordingly.

7. *Diversify your approach*: Diversify your approach to drive traffic to your website by using various channels such as social media, PR, influencer marketing, and other techniques.

Creating a viral website requires a significant amount of time, effort, and resources. It's not something that can be achieved overnight, and it requires a clear strategy, consistent content creation, and a strong understanding of the target audience.

Tools

There are a variety of tools that can help you build your website. Here are a few examples:

1.	**WordPress**: WordPress is a content management system (CMS) that allows you to create a website without needing to know how to code. It's free to use, but you will need to pay for hosting and domain name. Hosting can range from a few dollars a month to a few hundred dollars a month and domain names typically cost around $10 - $15 per year.

2.	**Wix**: Wix is a website builder that allows you to create a website using a drag-and-drop interface. It's free to use, but you can upgrade to a premium plan for additional features and to remove Wix branding. Premium plans start at $7.50 per month.

3.	**Squarespace**: Squarespace is a website builder that offers a variety of templates and design tools to create a professional-looking website. It starts from $12 per month.

4.	**Shopify**: Shopify is an e-commerce platform that allows you to create an online store and sell products. It starts from $29 per month.

5.	**Webflow**: Webflow is a website design tool that allows you to create a website using a visual editor. It starts from $14 per month.

These are just a few examples of the many tools available to help you build your website. Conducting thorough research and selecting the option that aligns with your specific needs and budget is of utmost importance. You'll also need to consider other tools such as analytics; marketing and SEO tools that can help you track and improve the performance of your website.

Promote through social media

Using social media to promote your viral website can be an effective way to drive traffic to your website and increase brand awareness. Here are some ideas:

1.   *Create a social media presence*: Set up accounts on the major social media platforms (such as Facebook, Twitter, Instagram, TikTok, and LinkedIn) that are relevant to your target audience.

2.   *Share high-quality content*: Share high-quality content that is relevant to your target audience and is likely to be shared by others. Use a mix of text, images, and videos to keep your followers engaged.

3.   *Use Hashtags*: Use relevant hashtags to increase the visibility of your content and make it easier for people to find your posts.

4.   *Engage with your followers*: Respond to comments and messages, and engage with other users by sharing and commenting on their posts.

5.   *Run social media ads*: Consider running targeted social media ads to reach a wider audience, and drive traffic to your website.

6.   *Collaborate with influencers*: Consider working with influencers in your niche to promote your website and reach a wider audience.

7.   *Track your results*: Use social media analytics tools to track the performance of your social media campaigns, and adjust your strategy accordingly.

Building a social media following takes time and effort, so be consistent and patient. You should also have a good understanding of your target audience, their behavior and what type of content they prefer.

Analytics tools

Social media analytics tools are used to track the performance of your social media campaigns and measure the impact of your efforts. Here are a few examples of popular social media analytics tools:

1.   **Hootsuite Insights**: This tool allows you to track key metrics such as engagement, reach, and follower growth for your social media accounts across multiple platforms. Hootsuite offers a free plan and paid plans starting from around $112 per month.

2.   **Sprout Social**: This tool allows you to track key metrics such as engagement, reach, and follower growth, and also allows you to schedule and publish content, and manage your social media accounts. Sprout Social offers a free trial and paid plans that start at $249 per month.

3.   **Google Analytics**: This tool allows you to track website traffic and conversions, including data on the source of your website visitors and how they interact with your website. Google Analytics is a free tool, but there are additional features and integrations available with a paid plan called Google Analytics 360, which starts at $150,000 per year.

4.   **Buzzsumo**: This tool allows you to track the performance of your content and also find out what kind of content is resonating with your target audience. Buzzsumo offers a free trial and paid plans that start at $199 per month.

5.   **Buffer**: This tool allows you to schedule, publish and track the performance of your social media accounts and also gives you

insights about your audience. Buffer offers a free plan and paid plans that start at $6 per month.

6.   **Iconosquare**: This tool allows you to track the performance of your Instagram account, including metrics such as engagement, reach, and follower growth. Iconosquare offers a free trial and paid plans that start at $49 per month.

7.   **Agorapulse**: This tool allows you to track the performance of your social media accounts, schedule and publish content, and manage your social media accounts. Agorapulse offers a free trial and paid plans that start at around $52 per month.

These are some examples of the many social media analytics tools available. You will need to research different options and choose the one that best fits your needs and budget. You should also consider integrating your social media analytics with your website analytics to get a more complete picture of your online performance and user behavior.

Have in mind that all this information can change over time, therefore always check on the provider's website about their prices.

Free analytics tools

There are several free social media analytics tools available. Here are a few examples:

1.   **Facebook Insights**: Facebook offers a built-in analytics tool called Facebook Insights, which allows you to track engagement and reach on your Facebook page.

2.   **Twitter Analytics**: Twitter offers a built-in analytics tool called Twitter Analytics, which allows you to track engagement and reach on your Twitter account.

3.   **Instagram Insights**: Instagram offers a built-in analytics tool called Instagram Insights, which allows you to track engagement and reach on your Instagram account.

4.   **YouTube Analytics**: YouTube offers a built-in analytics tool called YouTube Analytics, which allows you to track engagement and reach on your YouTube channel.

5.   **Google Analytics**: Google Analytics is a free tool that allows you to track website traffic and conversions, including data on the source of your website visitors and how they interact with your website.

6.   **Open Web Analytics**: Open Web Analytics is an open-source analytics tool that allows you to track website traffic, conversions, and user behavior.

7.   **Matomo**: formerly Piwik is an open-source analytics tool that allows you to track website traffic, conversions, and user behavior.

These tools are a good start to tracking your social media performance and website engagement and can be a good option if you're on a tight budget. They may not provide as much detail or functionality as paid tools, but they should give you a good idea of how your social media campaigns and website are performing.

Free and paid tools

Here is a list of free and paid tools that can help you with analytics, marketing, and SEO:

1.   <u>Analytics:</u>

•   Google Analytics (free)

- Matomo (free, open-source)
- OpenWeb Analytics (free, open-source)
- Adobe Analytics (paid)
- Mixpanel (paid)

2.   Marketing:
- MailChimp (free for small lists)
- Constant Contact (paid)
- Hootsuite (free and paid plans)
- Sprout Social (paid)
- Buffer (free and paid plans)

3.   SEO:
- Google Search Console (free)
- SEMrush (paid)
- Ahrefs (paid)
- Moz (paid)
- Keywords Everywhere (free and paid)

It's good to research different options and choose the ones that best fit your needs and budget. You should also consider the cost of other tools such as website analytics tools, email marketing tools, and other marketing tools that will be needed to achieve your goals.

Examples of viral websites

You can have a look at these viral websites that you can research to gain insights and inspiration for your own website:

1.   **BuzzFeed**: BuzzFeed is a popular website that creates and curates viral content across a wide range of topics including entertainment, news, and lifestyle.

2.   **The Huffington Post**: The Huffington Post is a news and opinion website that covers a wide range of topics, including politics, entertainment, lifestyle, and technology.

3.   **Tasty**: Tasty is a popular food website that creates and curates viral recipe videos, cooking tips, and food-related content.

4.   **9GAG**: 9GAG is a viral website that creates and curates content in the form of memes, GIFs, and other viral media.

5.   **Viral Nova**: Viral Nova is a viral website that creates and curates content in the form of articles, videos, and images that are designed to be highly shareable.

6.   **The Daily Mail**: The Daily Mail is a British news website that is known for its viral articles, celebrity news, and scandalous headlines.

These are just a few examples of viral websites, it's important to research different options and choose the one that best fits your niche and audience. You can also look for viral websites in your niche to gain insights and inspiration for your own website.

Creating interesting articles

Creating interesting articles in your niche requires a combination of creativity, research, and an understanding of your target audience. Here are a few tips to help you create interesting articles in your niche:

1.   *Understand your audience*: Understand your target audience, their interests, and what kind of content they are looking for. Utilize this information to develop content that deeply connects with your target audience.

2.   *Research your topic*: Conduct thorough research on your topic to ensure that your content is accurate, up-to-date, and informative. Use a variety of sources such as industry reports, expert interviews, and case studies.

3.   *Use storytelling*: Use storytelling techniques to make your content more engaging and interesting. Use anecdotes, examples, and case studies to illustrate your points and make your content more relatable.

4.   *Use visuals*: Use images, videos, infographics, and other forms of visual content to make your articles more engaging and interesting.

5.   *Keep it simple*: Write in a clear and concise style, using simple language and avoiding jargon. Enhance the readability of your text by incorporating headings and bullet points to make it easier to read.

6.   *Optimize for SEO*: Optimize your articles for search engines by including relevant keywords, meta descriptions, and alt tags for images.

7.   *Be original*: Create original and unique content that stands out from the competition. Offer new insights and perspectives on your topic.

8.   *Encourage engagement*: Encourage engagement by asking questions, creating polls, and asking for feedback.

It takes time and effort, so you have to be consistent and patient. You need also a good understanding of your target audience, their behavior, and what type of content they prefer.

Monetization

There are several ways to monetize your website, some of the most common ways include:

1.   *Advertising*: One of the most common ways to monetize a website is by displaying ads on your site. You can use platforms like Google AdSense or Media.net to place ads on your site and earn money when visitors click on them.

2.   *Affiliate marketing*: You can monetize your website by promoting other people's products or services and earning a commission for each sale or referral.

3.   *Sponsored content*: You can also monetize your website by creating sponsored content for brands. This can include sponsored blog posts, product reviews, or sponsored social media posts.

4.   *E-commerce*: If you have a website that sells products, you can monetize it by offering products and services to your audience.

5.   *Subscription*: You can monetize your website by offering exclusive content, access to a community, or other benefits to paying subscribers.

6.   *Consulting or coaching*: If you have expertise in a certain field, you can monetize your website by offering consulting or coaching services to your audience.

7.   *Lead generation*: If you have a website that attracts a lot of visitors, you can monetize it by collecting leads and selling them to other businesses.

The best way to monetize your website will depend on the type of website you have, your target audience, and your goals. You can use a combination of different monetization methods to maximize your revenue. You also have to consider the cost of running and maintaining your website, as well as the time and effort required to implement each monetization method.

Conclusion

Creating a viral website requires a clear strategy, consistent content creation, and a strong understanding of the target audience. Creating a viral website requires a substantial investment of time, effort, and resources. To create a viral website, you should start by defining your target audience, developing a content strategy, building a visually appealing and user-friendly website, optimizing for SEO, and promoting your website through various channels like social media and email marketing. You need to have a good understanding of the tools available to you such as website building, analytics, and marketing tools. To monetize your website, you have different options like advertising, affiliate marketing, sponsored content, e-commerce, subscription, consulting, and lead generation. The best way to monetize your website will depend on the type of website you have, your target audience, and your goals. Remember that creating a viral website is not something that can be achieved overnight; it requires patience, dedication, and a willingness to learn and adapt.

#20

Becoming A Transcriptionist

Transcribing Triumphs

Transcription means to convert recorded audio into written text. It is a valuable skill in today's workforce, as it allows for the creation of written records of meetings, interviews, and other spoken content. Transcription can be done remotely, making it a flexible job option. Furthermore, it is a good job option because it doesn't require a lot of education or experience to get started, and the demand for transcription services is high in many industries, such as legal, medical, and media. The rise of remote work and the increasing prevalence of digital audio and video recordings have led to an increase in the need for transcription services, making it a promising field for those looking for a new career opportunity.

Skillset

To become a transcriptionist, you will need the following skills:

1.   *Strong listening and comprehension skills*: As a transcriptionist, you will be listening to audio recordings and transcribing them into written text, so you need to have good listening skills and be able to understand different dialects and accents.

2.   *Excellent typing skills*: You will need to be able to type quickly and accurately in order to transcribe audio recordings in a timely manner.

3.   *Familiarity with transcription software*: Many transcriptionists use software programs to help them transcribe audio recordings. Familiarity with these programs will be helpful.

4.   *Attention to detail*: Transcription requires paying attention to every word spoken, punctuation, and sometimes specific terminology, so attention to detail is essential.

5.   *Strong language skills*: Transcriptionists should be fluent in the language they are transcribing.

6.   *Good organizational skills*: Transcription work can be repetitive and time-consuming, so you will have to keep track of your progress and stay organized.

7.   *Understanding of legal or medical terminologies* (if you want to transcribe legal or medical audio).

8.   *Familiarity with common file formats and audio quality standards*.

9.   *Flexibility and Adaptability*: As transcription work can be a bit monotonous, you will need to have the ability to adapt to different types of audio and styles of speech, as well as be able to multitask and handle multiple projects at a time.

By developing these skills, you can increase your chances of becoming a transcriptionist.

Software programs and how much they cost

There are several software programs that transcriptionists use to help them transcribe audio recordings. Some of the most popular include:

1. **Express Scribe** (https://www.nch.com.au/scribe/index.html): This is free transcription software that allows you to control the playback of audio recordings using a foot pedal or keyboard shortcuts. It also includes a built-in word processor and can handle a variety of file formats. You can also upgrade to a professional version for more functions and flexibility.

2. **InqScribe** (https://www.inqscribe.com/): This software allows for the transcription of video as well as audio and has a built-in media player, making it easy to play, pause, and rewind audio. It also includes a set of tools for editing and annotating transcripts. It costs $99 for a one-time purchase.

3. **Transcribe** (https://transcribe.wreally.com/): This is web-based transcription software that allows you to upload audio or video files and transcribe them directly in your browser. It also has a variety of features such as variable playback speed, automatic timestamps, and the ability to export transcripts in different file formats. It costs $20/month for individual use and 20/month + $6/hour for automatic transcription.

4. **oTranscribe** (https://otranscribe.com/): This is a free, open-source transcription software that runs in your browser, with a simple interface and basic features such as variable playback speed, automatic timestamps, and the ability to export transcripts in different file formats.

5.   **Sonix** (https://sonix.ai/): This is cloud-based transcription software that uses AI to transcribe audio and video files. It has a variety of features such as automatic timestamps, speaker identification, and the ability to export transcripts in different file formats. It starts from $10/hour for pay as you go projects and $5/hour + $22/month per user for teams.

As you can see, some of the software is free, while others require a monthly or one-time payment. It's worth trying out a few different options to see which one works best for you and your needs.

Typing speed and how to achieve it

The typing speed required to become a transcriptionist can vary depending on the employer or client. Some may require a minimum typing speed of 60 words per minute (WPM), while others may require a speed of 80 WPM or higher. A higher typing speed can be beneficial as it will allow you to transcribe audio recordings more quickly and efficiently.

To achieve a high typing speed, you can practice typing regularly and use typing software to track your progress. Some popular typing software includes:

1.   **TypingClub** (https://www.typingclub.com/): This is free typing software that includes a variety of typing lessons and games to help you improve your typing speed and accuracy.

2.   **Typing** (https://www.typing.com/): This website offers typing lessons for beginners and advanced users, and allows you to track your progress and set typing goals.

3.   **Nitro Type** (https://www.nitrotype.com/): This is a typing game that allows you to race against other users and track your progress.

4.   **10FastFingers**   (https://10fastfingers.com/typing-test/english): This website offers typing tests in different languages, and allows you to track your typing speed and accuracy over time.

In addition to using typing software, you can also practice typing on your own. Try typing out emails, articles or any other written content to improve your speed and accuracy.

Typing speed is not the only requirement to become a transcriptionist, accuracy is also a key factor. You should strive for both, typing speed and accuracy. With regular practice, you can improve your typing speed and increase your chances of getting hired as a transcriptionist.

You can also look for free typing certificates on Google. You can take a test; you can retake it until you achieve the desired speed. You can then attach this certificate to your resume when applying for jobs.

Companies and websites

There are many companies and websites that hire work-from-home transcriptionists. Some of the most reputable and trusted include:

1.   **Rev** (https://www.rev.com/): Rev is a well-known and reputable transcription and captioning company that hires work-

from-home transcriptionists. They offer flexible work hours and competitive pay.

2. **TranscribeMe** (https://www.transcribeme.com/): TranscribeMe is another popular transcription company that hires work-from-home transcriptionists. They offer a variety of audio and video transcription projects, and they pay per audio hour.

3. **GoTranscript** (https://gotranscript.com/): GoTranscript is a transcription and translation company that hires work-from-home transcriptionists. They offer flexible work hours and competitive pay.

4. **Scribie** (https://scribie.com/): Scribie is a transcription company that hires work-from-home transcriptionists. They offer a variety of audio and video transcription projects, and they pay per audio hour.

5. **Tigerfish** (https://tigerfish.com/): Tigerfish is a transcription company that hires work-from-home transcriptionists. They offer a variety of audio and video transcription projects, and they pay per audio hour.

6. **AccuTran Global** (https://www.accutranglobal.com/): AccuTran Global is a transcription company that hires work-from-home transcriptionists. They offer a variety of audio and video transcription projects, and they pay per audio hour.

7. **Daily Transcription** (https://dailytranscription.com/careers/): Daily Transcription is another website that hires transcriptionists on work from home basis, but it is only for people that are based in the USA.

These are just a few examples of companies and websites that hire work-from-home transcriptionists. These companies may have different requirements, so check their websites for more information on the application process and qualifications.

Earning potential

The pay for work-from-home transcriptionists can vary depending on the company and the type of transcription work. Some companies pay per audio hour, while others pay per word or per line. Some companies pay on a project-by-project basis, while others offer a regular salary or hourly wage. The pay can also vary depending on the experience, qualifications, and typing speed of the transcriptionist.

For example, Rev pays its transcriptionists between $0.36 and $1.25 per audio minute, depending on the quality of work. TranscribeMe pays its transcriptionists around $15 to $22 per audio hour. GoTranscript pays its transcriptionists between $0.60 and $1.20 per audio minute. Scribie pays $10 per audio hour; Daily Transcription pays $0.75 to $1.50 per audio minute. Tigerfish pays $0.005 to $0.0066 per word and AccuTran Global pays $0.005 to $0.0075 per word.

Pay rates can fluctuate and change over time, so it's a good idea to check the company's website or contact them directly for the most up-to-date information on pay rates.

Some companies may have different requirements, such as a minimum typing speed, a certain number of hours of availability per week, or a set of qualifications. Therefore, make sure to check their website for all the up-to-date information.

Conclusion

Becoming a transcriptionist is a great way to enter the world of remote work, and it can be a great option for those with good listening and typing skills. It is a field that can be flexible, in terms of hours and location, and can be a great option for those who want to work from home. It is a good job option because it doesn't require a lot of education or experience to get started. The demand for transcription services is high in many industries, such as legal, medical, and media. To be successful in this field, it is important to have a good typing speed and accuracy, as well as good listening skills and attention to detail. It is also beneficial to be familiar with transcription software and to have knowledge of legal or medical terminologies if you are looking to transcribe that type of audio. With the right skills and dedication, you can be on your way to becoming a successful transcriptionist.

#21

Create A Membership Website

Your Online Community

A membership site is a great way to monetize content or services and build a community of loyal customers. It allows you to restrict access to certain content or features on your website to only paying members. To create a membership site, you will need to choose a platform or software, set up a payment system, and determine the content or services you will offer to members. It's also important to consider the user experience and make it easy for members to navigate and access the content they have paid for. You should have a clear and compelling value proposition for your potential members. With a solid plan and the right tools, you can create a successful membership site that generates recurring revenue for your business.

Is this for you?

A membership site is ideal for businesses or individuals who have a steady stream of valuable content or services to offer, and who want to monetize that content or services by charging for access. This can be:

•   Online course creators

•   Content creators (bloggers, podcasters, YouTubers)

- Coaches and consultants

- Service providers (such as graphic designers, copywriters)

- Subscription-based product sellers

- Communities and networking groups

- Non-profit organizations

It's also a great option for business owners who want to build a community of loyal customers and provide additional perks or benefits to members.

Skillset

To create and run a successful membership site, certain skills are necessary:

1.   **Technical skills**: Depending on the platform or software you choose, you may need to have a basic understanding of website development and design, as well as the ability to integrate payment systems and set up membership levels.

2.   **Marketing and sales skills**: You will need to be able to promote your membership site and effectively communicate the value proposition to potential members.

3.   **Content creation skills**: If you plan to offer exclusive content to members, you will need to have the ability to create high-quality, engaging content that is relevant to your target audience.

4.   **Project management skills**: Running a membership site requires organization and time management to ensure that you are able to consistently deliver new content and manage member queries.

5.   **Customer service skills**: As your membership site grows, you will need to be able to handle customer service inquiries and resolve any issues that may arise.

6.   **Financial skills**: You'll need to keep track of revenue, expenses, and budgeting for your membership site, you should also have knowledge on how to run a profitable business.

It's not necessary to be an expert in all of these areas, but having a basic understanding of each will be helpful in running a successful membership site.

Time

The amount of time required getting a membership site up and running will vary depending on several factors such as:

•   **The complexity of the site**: A simple membership site with a few levels and basic content may take less time to set up than a more complex site with multiple levels, integrations, and a large amount of exclusive content.

•   **Your technical skill level**: If you already have experience with website development, it may take less time to set up your membership site than if you are starting from scratch.

- **Your content creation**: How much exclusive content you need to create and how much time it takes to create it will also play a role.

On average, you should expect to spend several weeks to a few months setting up and launching your membership site. With a clear plan, the right tools, and a dedicated effort, it is possible to get a basic membership site up and running within a few weeks.

Creating a membership site is an ongoing process and it will take ongoing time and effort to manage and grow it.

How to price your membership website?

Pricing your membership website is an important decision that can have a significant impact on your revenue and the success of your site. Here is what to consider when figuring out your pricing structure:

1. **Value**: The price of your membership should be directly tied to the value that your site provides to members. Make sure that the benefits of your site outweigh the cost for your members.

2. **Competitors**: Research your competitors and see what they are charging for similar membership sites. This will give you an idea of the general price range for your niche.

3. **Costs**: Consider the costs of running your site, such as hosting, payment processing fees, and content creation. Your pricing should be high enough to cover these costs and generate a profit.

4.   **Tiers**: Offer different levels of membership at different price points, for example, a basic membership and a premium membership. This allows members to choose a level that fits their budget and needs.

5.   **Test**: Start with a price that you believe is fair and reasonable, and test it out by running a promotion or offering a limited-time discount. Monitor the results and adjust your pricing if necessary.

6.   **Flexibility**: Allow members to purchase memberships on a recurring basis like monthly, quarterly, or annually, giving them the flexibility to choose the option that works best for them.

Ultimately, the key to pricing your membership website is to strike a balance between providing value to your members and generating revenue for your business.

Sign up for a membership site yourself

It can be a good idea to sign up for a membership site yourself, as it can give you valuable insights into the user experience and help you identify any potential issues or areas for improvement. By becoming a member, you can see first-hand how easy it is to navigate the site, access content, and interact with other members.

By signing up as a member, you can also gain a deeper understanding of your target audience and their needs, which can help you improve the content and features offered on your site.

It's also important to have a clear perspective and not to get too influenced by the features or benefits offered by the competitors, since it's easy to get caught up on what others are doing and lose focus on your own unique value proposition.

As the owner of the membership site, you will have access to all the data, analytics and customer feedback and that can be more valuable than the experience of being just a member.

Get to know your members

Getting to know your members is an important part of running a successful membership site, as it allows you to understand their needs and tailor your content and services to meet those needs. Here are some ways to get to know your members:

1.   **Surveys**: Send out regular surveys to your members to gather feedback and information about their interests, needs, and preferences.

2.   **Communication**: Encourage open communication between members and the site's staff or owner, and make sure to respond to member inquiries and feedback in a timely and professional manner.

3.   **Analytics**: Use web analytics tools to track member behavior on your site, such as which pages they visit and how much time they spend on the site.

4.   **Social Media**: Utilize social media platforms to connect with your members and understand their interests, likes and dislikes.

5.   **Community**: Encourage members to interact with one another through forums, chats, or other community-building features on your site.

6.   **Testimonials**: Ask members to provide testimonials or reviews of your site, this can give you a good understanding of what they like and dislike about your site and what you can improve.

7.   **Personal touch**: A personal touch can always help to build a strong relationship, such as sending a birthday email, or a personalized message on their membership anniversary, this shows that you care about them and value their membership. For example, you could attach a discount code for one time purchase of some item you are selling on your website.

By utilizing these methods, you can gain valuable insights into your members and use that information to improve your site and retain members.

Improving your site

Improving your membership site over time is essential for retaining members and attracting new ones. Here are few examples of how to improve your site:

1.   **Listen to feedback**: Regularly gather feedback from your members and take their suggestions and complaints into consideration when making changes to your site.

2.   **Analyze data**: Use web analytics tools to track member behavior on your site and identify areas where improvements can be made.

3.   **Add new content**: Regularly add new and relevant content to your site to keep members engaged and attract new members.

4.   **Update design**: Regularly update the design of your site to keep it looking fresh and modern.

5.   **Increase engagement**: Encourage member engagement by adding interactive features such as forums, chats, or live webinars.

6.   **Optimize for mobile**: Ensure that your site is optimized for mobile devices, as more and more people access the internet from their smartphones.

7.   **Personalization**: Use data you have collected about your members to personalize the experience for them, this can help to increase engagement and retention.

8.   **Test and measure**: Continuously test and measure new features, pricing, and promotions to see what works best for your members and your business.

By regularly improving your site and listening to feedback from your members, you can ensure that your site stays relevant and valuable to them, which will ultimately lead to increased engagement and retention.

Making money

Making money with a membership site is about providing value to your members and monetizing that value. Here is how to monetize your membership website:

1.   **Subscription-based access**: Charge a monthly or annual fee for access to your exclusive content or services.

2.   **Upsells**: Offer additional services or products to members at an additional cost, such as coaching, e-books, consulting or personalized services.

3.   **Advertising**: Partner with other businesses to promote their products or services to your members.

4.   **Affiliate marketing**: Partner with other businesses to promote their products or services to your members and earn a commission on sales.

5.   **Sponsorships**: Partner with other businesses to sponsor your site and gain access to your members.

6.   **Premium content**: Offer premium content to members who are willing to pay more for access to exclusive content or features.

7.   **Event & Webinars**: Organize paid events and webinars for your members and charge for attendance.

Making money with a membership site is about finding a balance between providing values to your members and monetizing that value in a way that doesn't negatively impact the user experience.

You should consider the costs of running the site, such as hosting, payment processing fees, content creation, and customer service, and make sure that the revenue generated from your membership site covers those costs and generates a profit.

Tools to help you build a membership website

There are several tools available to help you build and manage a membership website. Some popular options include:

WordPress plugins: There are a variety of WordPress plugins available that can help you restrict access to certain pages or content on your site, manage member accounts and payments, and more. Some popular ones are WooCommerce Memberships, MemberPress, and Restrict Content Pro.

Platforms: There are also platforms specifically designed for building membership sites, such as Kajabi, Thinkific, and Memberful. These platforms typically offer a wide range of features and integrations that can help you manage your site, such as content delivery, membership levels, and payment processing.

Payment processors: You will also need a payment processor to handle member payments. Some options include Stripe, PayPal, and Square.

Email marketing: Email marketing tools like Mailchimp, Constant Contact, Aweber, etc can help you to communicate and keep in touch with your members.

Analytic tools: Google Analytics, Mixpanel, etc are some of the popular tools to track and analyze the data of the users and help you to make data-driven decisions.

Community building tools: Tools like Slack, Discord, and Circle can help you to create and manage a community for your members to interact and share their thoughts.

Research and compare the features of different tools to find the one that best fits your needs and budget.

Cost

The cost of Kajabi, Thinkific, and Memberful will vary depending on the plan and features you choose. Here is a general overview of the pricing plans for each platform:

Kajabi: Kajabi has four different pricing plans, starting at $149/month. The plans include different features such as email marketing, webinars, and affiliate management. Kajabi offers a 14-day free trial, and all plans come with a 30-day money-back guarantee.

Thinkific: Thinkific has four pricing plans, starting at $39/month. The plans include different features such as course creation tools, integrations, and payment processing. Thinkific also offers a free plan, which includes basic features, and a 14-day free trial for all paid plans.

Memberful: Memberful has a simple pricing structure; it charges a flat rate of $25/month + 4.9% transaction fee. This pricing structure is flexible and scalable. It has a free plan $0/month + 10% transaction fee.

These are just general pricing information and some plans may have additional costs such as transaction fees, or additional charges for certain features. It's always a good idea to check the pricing page of these platforms and compare it with other alternatives, to find the one that best fits your needs and budget.

WordPress plugins

There are many WordPress plugins available that can help you build a membership website, but some of the best options include:

MemberPress: MemberPress is a popular and powerful plugin that allows you to easily create and manage membership levels, restrict access to content, and manage payments. It offers a wide range of features, including integration with popular payment processors, drip content, and affiliate management. MemberPress offers a few different pricing plans, starting at $179.50 per year for a single site license. The plans include different features such as integration with popular payment processors, drip content, and affiliate management. A 14-day money-back guarantee is also included.

WooCommerce Memberships: This plugin allows you to sell memberships to your site using the popular WooCommerce plugin. It includes features such as membership plans, content dripping, and email reminders. WooCommerce Memberships is a free plugin but you will need to pay for the WooCommerce plugin to use it. The cost for the WooCommerce plugin is $16.59/month for the core plugin, but you will need to pay for additional add-ons and extensions as needed.

Restrict Content Pro: Restrict Content Pro is a user-friendly plugin that allows you to easily create membership levels and restrict access to content. It includes features such as integration with popular payment processors, discounted pricing for members, and detailed reporting. Restrict Content Pro offers a few different pricing plans, starting at $99 per year for a single site license. The plans include different features such as integration with popular payment processors, discounted pricing for members, and detailed reporting. There is also a 30-day money-back guarantee.

s2Member: s2Member is a free membership plugin that allows you to easily create membership levels, restrict access to content, and manage payments. It offers a wide range of features, including integration with popular payment processors, drip content, and detailed reporting. s2Member is a free plugin, you will not have to pay for the plugin itself, and however, you may have to pay for additional add-ons and features if you need them. The plugin has also a paid version priced at $89 one-time payment offering pro features.

Magic Members: Magic Members is a plugin that allows you to easily create membership levels, restrict access to content, and manage payments. It includes features such as integration with popular payment processors, drip content, and detailed reporting. Magic Members offers a few different pricing plans, starting at $97 for a single site license. The plans include different features such as integration with popular payment processors, drip content, and detailed reporting. A 30-day money-back guarantee is also included.

These are some of the most popular and widely used WordPress membership plugins, they are known to be reliable and have a great support community. As with any plugin, it's always a good idea to research, compare features, and test the plugin before you make a decision and install it on your website.

It's always a good idea to check the pricing page of these plugins and compare it with other alternatives, to find the one that best fits your needs and budget.

Drip content

Drip content refers to the practice of releasing content to members on a schedule rather than all at once. Drip content allows you to release new content to your members over time, which can help to keep them engaged and coming back to your site.

It's a feature offered by some membership plugins and platforms, it allows you to set a schedule for when different pieces of content will be released to your members. For example, you can release a new lesson or module of a course each week, or release a new piece of content each day.

It is a useful feature for membership sites that offer courses, training programs, or other types of content that are meant to be consumed over time. It also helps to keep members engaged and coming back to the site, as they have something new to look forward to.

Drip content also allows you to create a sense of urgency and scarcity, which can help to increase conversions, and make members feel they are getting a good value for the money they pay.

Drip content is a feature that allows you to release content to members on a schedule, it's useful for membership sites that offer courses, training programs, or other types of content that are meant to be consumed over time. It also helps to keep members engaged and coming back to the site, as they have something new to look forward to.

Conclusion

In conclusion, creating a membership website can be a rewarding venture, providing a platform to share valuable content, build a community, and generate revenue. It offers the opportunity to connect with like-minded individuals, offer exclusive benefits, and establish a sustainable business model.

When setting up a membership site, it is important to consider the target audience and their needs, as well as the skills required to develop and maintain the site. Pricing the membership appropriately is crucial, striking a balance between affordability for members and sustainability for your business.

To succeed in the long term, continuous improvement is essential. Gathering feedback, analyzing data, and adapting your site over time will help enhance the member experience and retain their loyalty.

The success of your membership site ultimately relies on the value you provide to your members. Engaging content, personalized experiences and a strong sense of community will keep members coming back and attract new ones. With careful planning, ongoing refinement, and a commitment to member satisfaction, your membership site has the potential to thrive and fulfill its intended purpose.

#22

Create WordPress Themes

WordPress Wonders

Creating a WordPress theme involves designing and building the visual layout and functionality of a website using the WordPress content management system. This can include designing the header, footer, and sidebar, as well as the overall color scheme and typography. It also involves creating templates for different types of pages and posts, such as the home page, single post page, and archive pages. To create a WordPress theme, you will need a basic understanding of HTML, CSS, and PHP, as well as experience with the WordPress platform. You can use tools such as Adobe Photoshop or Sketch to design the layout and create the necessary image assets. Once your theme is complete, you can make it available for others to use on their own WordPress sites.

Is this for you?

Creating a WordPress theme is ideal for web designers and developers who have experience with HTML, CSS, and PHP, and are familiar with the WordPress platform. It is also ideal for those who want to create custom designs for their own website or for clients. It's a great way for developers to showcase their skills and build a portfolio. If someone is looking for a way to monetize their skills and earn income, creating and selling WordPress themes can be a viable option.

Skillset

To create a WordPress theme, you will need a good understanding of the following skills:

1.   *HTML*: You should be proficient in writing HTML code to structure the content of your website.

2.   *CSS*: You should be comfortable with CSS to control the layout and presentation of your website.

3.   *PHP*: You should have a good understanding of the PHP programming language, as WordPress themes are built using PHP templates.

4.   *WordPress*: You should be familiar with the WordPress platform, including its template hierarchy and the use of actions and filters.

5.   *Design*: You should have a good sense of design and be able to create visually appealing layouts.

6.   *Responsive Design*: Your theme should be responsive which means it should adapt to different screen sizes and devices, so you should be comfortable with creating responsive layouts.

7.   *Graphic design*: Tools like Adobe Photoshop or Sketch can be used to design the layout and create the necessary image assets.

8.   *Debugging*: You should be comfortable with debugging your code to troubleshoot any issues that may arise during the development process.

Having good problem solving skills and attention to details are also important.

If you want to monetize your theme, you should have some knowledge about how to sell and market your theme.

Conduct market research

Conducting market research for a WordPress theme can help you identify the needs and preferences of your target audience, and ensure that your theme will be well-received by potential customers. Here are some steps you can take to conduct market research for your WordPress theme:

1.   *Identify your target audience.* Find out what are their needs and preferences. You can use tools such as Google Analytics to gather demographic data about your website visitors.

2.   *Analyze the competition*: Take a look at other WordPress themes that are already available on the market. Analyze their features and pricing, as well as their strengths and weaknesses.

3.   *Study customer reviews*: Look for customer reviews on different WordPress theme marketplaces, forums and social media channels. Pay attention to common feedback, complaints and feature requests.

4.   *Identify trends and gaps in the market*: Look for any trends or gaps in the market that you can capitalize on. For example, if there are not many themes available for a specific niche, this could be an opportunity for you to create a theme that fills that gap.

5.   *Conduct surveys and interviews*: Reach out to your target audience and ask them directly about their needs and preferences.

You can conduct online surveys, or conduct interviews over the phone or in-person.

6.   *Look for inspiration*: Look for inspiration from other sources such as other platforms and industries, taking note of what works and what doesn't, what's popular and what's not.

By conducting market research, you will be able to create a theme that meets the needs of your target audience and stands out in the market.

Understand your audience

Understanding your audience is an important step in creating a successful WordPress theme. Here is how to understand your audience:

1.   *Identify demographics*: Gather information about your audience's age, gender, location, education, and income level. This can help you understand their needs and preferences.

2.   *Analyze website data*: Use tools such as Google Analytics to gather data about your website visitors. Look at the pages they visit, how long they stay on your site, and what actions they take.

3.   *Engage with your audience*: Engage with your audience on social media, forums, and other online platforms. Respond to comments, listen to feedback, and answer questions.

4.   *Look for patterns*: Look for patterns in the data and feedback you collect. Identify common needs and preferences among your audience.

By understanding your audience, you will be able to create a theme that meets their needs and speaks to them directly. This will make it more likely that they will purchase your theme and recommend it to others.

How to sell your WordPress themes?

Selling a WordPress theme can be a great way to monetize your skills and earn income. Here are some ways to sell your WordPress theme:

1.   **WordPress Theme Marketplaces**: There are several popular WordPress theme marketplaces such as:

Themeforest (https://themeforest.net/),

Creative Market (https://creativemarket.com/),

and MOJO Marketplace (https://www.mojomarketplace.com/),

where you can submit your theme for sale. These marketplaces have large audiences and can help you reach a wide range of potential customers.

2.   **Your own website**: You can also sell your themes directly from your own website. This can be a good option if you already have an established audience and want to have more control over the pricing and distribution of your theme.

3.   **Freelancing platforms**: Platforms such as Upwork, Freelancer and Fiverr can be used to find clients that are looking for custom WordPress themes.

4.   **Social Media**: You can use social media platforms such as Facebook, Twitter, and Instagram to promote your theme and drive traffic to your website or marketplace listings.

5.   **Paid Advertising**: You can use paid advertising such as Google Ads, Facebook Ads, and Instagram Ads to drive traffic to your website or marketplace listings.

6.   **Blogging and Content Marketing**: Creating content such as articles, tutorials, and videos related to WordPress theme development can help attract potential customers to your website.

When selling your theme, it's important to have a detailed and well-organized product page that highlights the key features and benefits of your theme. Use screenshots, videos, and a live demo to showcase the theme in action. Also make sure to have a clear and easy to use purchase process, and provide good customer support.

Conclusion

Creating and selling WordPress themes can be a rewarding endeavor for several reasons:

Monetization of Skills: If you have skills in web design and development, creating WordPress themes allows you to monetize those skills and turn your passion into a source of income. You can earn money by selling your themes and potentially generating passive income through ongoing sales.

Showcase Your Talent: Creating WordPress themes provides a platform for you to showcase your creativity, design skills, and technical expertise. It allows you to demonstrate your abilities to potential clients or employers and build a portfolio of impressive work.

Reach a Wide Audience: WordPress powers a significant portion of the internet, and there is a vast user base in need of attractive and functional themes. By selling your themes, you can reach a broad audience of website owners, bloggers, businesses, and individuals looking to enhance their online presence.

Continuous Demand: Websites are constantly being created, updated, and redesigned. This ongoing demand for themes means there is a steady market for your products. As long as you stay updated with the latest trends and continuously improve your offerings, you can maintain a sustainable business.

Creative Freedom: Creating WordPress themes allows you to unleash your creativity and design unique layouts and functionalities. You have the freedom to experiment with different styles, color schemes, and features, catering to various industries, niches, or personal preferences.

Community and Collaboration: The WordPress community is vast and supportive. By participating in this community, you can connect with like-minded individuals, collaborate on projects, and learn from others. Engaging with the community can help you grow as a developer and expand your network.

Creating and selling WordPress themes is a worthwhile pursuit that combines your skills, creativity, and business acumen. It offers a chance to earn income, showcase your talent, reach a wide audience, and be part of a thriving community.

#23

Rent Your Extra Space

Rental Profits

This is not exactly a "Make money online" method, but it worth mentioning, because if you have the space, you can easily create an extra revenue stream.

Renting out extra space in your home or property can be a great way to earn additional income. Whether you have a spare room, a basement, or a garage, you can put that space to use by renting it out to someone in need. The earning potential can vary depending on the location, size, and amenities of the space, but with the right pricing and marketing, you can potentially earn a significant amount of money. Renting out extra space can also provide a sense of security and companionship for those who may be looking for short-term or long-term housing.

Platforms

There are several online platforms available for renting out extra space in your home or property. Some of the most popular include:

1.   **Airbnb**: A platform that allows you to rent out your entire home, a private room, or shared space to travelers.

2.   **VRBO (Vacation Rentals By Owner)**: A platform that specializes in vacation rentals, including homes, apartments, and condos.

3.   **Booking.com**: A platform that allows you to list your property for short-term rentals and manage bookings and payments.

4.   **Roomster**: A platform that allows you to rent out a spare room in your home to a roommate.

5.   **SpareRoom**: A platform that allows you to rent out a spare room, a short-term rental, or a whole property.

These are some of the most popular platforms, but there are many other platforms available depending on your location and the type of space you want to rent. You can also list your space on classifieds websites like Craigslist, Facebook marketplaces, and other local classifieds websites.

Examples:

StowIt is a US-based self-storage and warehouse company that offers secure, climate-controlled storage options, including units for personal belongings, RVs, boats, and commercial use. Customers can conveniently access their items during operating hours and make online reservations and payments through the company's website.

Companies in Europe

Here are several European companies that offer a similar service where you can rent out extra space in your home or property and earn money through their platform. Here are a few examples:

1. **Storebox**: is a German company that provides self-storage solutions for both private and business customers. They allow individuals to rent out their extra space, such as garages, basements, or attics, to other people who need storage.

2. **SpaceWays**: is a UK-based company that allows homeowners to rent out their extra space, such as garages, sheds, and loft space, to people in need of storage.

3. **Boxie24**: is a German company that provides self-storage solutions for both private and business customers. They allow individuals to rent out their extra space, such as garages, basements, or attics, to other people who need storage.

These are few examples of European companies that offer this type of service, and there may be more options available depending on your location. Check the company's terms and conditions, as well as their insurance coverage, to ensure that you and your property are protected.

Conclusion

Renting out extra space in your home or property can be a great way to earn additional income and utilize unused space. There are many online platforms available that make it easy to list and manage your space, such as Airbnb, VRBO, Booking.com, Roomster, SpareRoom, and many others. You must consider the legal and tax implications of renting out your space, as well as the potential for wear and tear on your property. With the right pricing, marketing, and management, renting out extra space can be a profitable and fulfilling experience.

#24

A Facebook Page

Social Media Earnings

Starting a Facebook page is an easy and cost-effective way to reach a large audience and promote your business. By creating a page, you can connect with customers, share content, and build your brand. To make money with your Facebook page, you can use it to drive traffic to your website or online store, offer special promotions, or run Facebook ads. The importance of a Facebook page in developing your business lies in its ability to reach a broad audience, build brand awareness, and engage with customers. With over 2.7 billion monthly active users, Facebook is one of the largest and most effective platforms for marketing and advertising.

Is this for you?

A Facebook page is ideal for any business, organization, or individual looking to reach and engage with a large online audience. Whether you're a small business owner, freelancer, artist, non-profit, or any other type of entity, having a Facebook page can help you connect with customers, build brand awareness, and grow your audience. It is also suitable for individuals looking to establish a personal brand or promote a cause.

Skillset

To effectively manage a Facebook page, you need several skills including:

1.   *Content creation*: The ability to create engaging and shareable content, such as photos, videos, and written posts, is crucial for keeping your page active and growing your audience.

2.   *Social media strategy*: Developing a clear strategy for your page, including defining your target audience and setting goals, is important for making the most of your efforts.

3.   *Marketing and advertising*: Knowledge of how to promote your page and reach new audiences through Facebook's advertising platform can help you reach your goals more effectively.

4.   *Engagement*: Understanding how to engage with your audience by responding to comments, messages, and reviews, and creating a community around your page is key to success.

5.   *Analytics*: The ability to analyze data and track metrics such as page likes, engagement, and reach, will help you evaluate the effectiveness of your efforts and make informed decisions.

These skills can be learned through online courses, hands-on experience, and continuous education. It is also possible to delegate some tasks to a social media manager or marketing agency if necessary.

Time and money

The time and money you need to invest in your Facebook page will depend on your goals and resources. Here are some general guidelines:

1.   *Time investment*: Managing a Facebook page requires a consistent time investment, at least a few hours per week, to create and share content, respond to comments and messages, and monitor your page's performance.

2.   *Money investment*: Creating a Facebook page is free, but promoting your page through advertising can incur costs. The amount you need to invest in advertising will depend on your budget and advertising goals. Facebook offers options for both large and small budgets, and you can set a daily or lifetime budget for your ad campaign.

The more time and money you invest in your Facebook page, the more effective it will be in reaching your goals. It is also possible to achieve success with a limited budget and time commitment by prioritizing your efforts and being strategic in your approach.

People on Facebook

People visit Facebook for a variety of reasons, some of them are:

1.   *Connecting with friends and family*: Facebook is a social platform where people can connect with friends and family, share updates and news, and stay in touch.

2.   *Finding and joining communities*: Facebook allows users to discover and join groups based on common interests, such as hobbies, causes, and political views.

3.   *Discovering and sharing content*: Facebook is a source of news and entertainment, where users can discover and share articles, videos, and other forms of content.

4.   *Marketing and advertising*: Businesses and organizations use Facebook to reach and engage with customers, and to promote their products and services through advertising.

5.   *Staying informed*: Facebook is a source of information, where users can stay informed about current events and trending topics.

All in all, people visit Facebook to connect, engage, and be informed. Whether it's for personal or professional reasons, Facebook provides a platform for people to share and discover content, build communities, and connect with others.

Research your niche

To research your niche on Facebook, you can follow these steps:

1.   *Search for related pages*: Use the Facebook search bar to find pages related to your niche. Look for pages with large followings, high engagement, and a focus on your target audience.

2.   *Join groups*: Join groups related to your niche to see what type of content is being shared and what topics are being

discussed. This can give you an insight into what your target audience is interested in.

3.   *Analyze page metrics*: Use Facebook's Page Insights to analyze the performance of pages in your niche. This includes metrics such as page views, engagement, and demographics, which can help you, understand your target audience and what types of content are performing well.

4.   *Monitor competitor pages*: Keep an eye on the pages of your competitors to see what types of content they are posting, what is resonating with their audience, and what types of engagement they are receiving.

5.   *Surveys and polls*: Use Facebook's polling and survey tools to gather data directly from your target audience. Ask questions about their interests, preferences, and opinions to gain a deeper understanding of your niche.

By conducting research, you can gain a better understanding of your niche, your target audience, and what types of content are resonating with them on Facebook. This can help you tailor your approach and create more effective content for your page.

Create engaging posts

To create engaging posts on Facebook, follow these tips:

1.   *Know your audience*: Understand your target audience's interests, preferences, and pain points. Develop content that deeply

resonates with your audience and effectively addresses their specific needs and concerns.

2.   *Use visuals*: Posts with images and videos tend to receive more engagement than text-only posts. Ensure that your visuals are of superior quality and directly relevant to the content you are presenting. Ask questions: Encourage engagement by asking questions and starting conversations. Ask for opinions, thoughts, or feedback on a topic.

3.   *Share personal stories*: Personal stories and anecdotes can be highly engaging and help to build a connection with your audience.

4.   *Utilize humor*: Adding humor to your posts can make them more shareable and increase engagement.

5.   *Offer value*: Share useful tips, insights, or resources that can add value to your audience's lives.

6.   *Use calls to action*: Encourage engagement by including calls to action, such as asking people to like, share, or comment on your post.

This way, you can increase engagement and build a stronger connection with your audience on Facebook. It's also important to experiment and find what works best for your audience and niche.

Use your personal profile in your advantage

Your personal Facebook profile can be an asset in promoting your business or personal brand if used effectively. Here are some ways to use your personal Facebook profile to your advantage:

1.	*Establish yourself as an expert*: Share valuable information and insights related to your industry or niche, and engage with others in the industry by commenting on their posts.

2.	*Connect with potential customers*: Reach out to potential customers, clients, and partners by sending friend requests and private messages.

3.	*Network with industry professionals*: Attend industry events, join groups and participate in discussions related to your niche, and connect with other industry professionals.

4.	*Share your business content*: Share content from your business page, such as blog posts, promotions, and events, to reach a larger audience.

5.	*Personal branding*: Use your personal profile to showcase your personality and brand, by sharing personal stories, experiences, and achievements.

By leveraging your personal Facebook profile, you can increase your visibility, build relationships, and promote your business or personal brand. Just remember to keep a balance between personal and professional content, and to maintain a professional image on your profile.

Monetize

Here are different ways how to monetize your Facebook page:

1.   *Sponsored content*: Partner with brands to create sponsored content for your page. This can include sponsored posts, reviews, or promotions.

2.   *Affiliate marketing*: Share affiliate links for products or services related to your niche. You'll earn a commission for each sale or lead generated through your link.

3.   *Ad revenue*: Place ads on your Facebook page, either through Facebook's ad platform or by working with a third-party ad network.

4.   *Selling products*: Use your Facebook page to promote and sell your own products, either through Facebook's Marketplace or through a third-party e-commerce platform.

5.   *Offering services*: Use your Facebook page to promote and sell your services, such as consulting, coaching, or training.

6.   *Crowdfunding*: Utilize Facebook's fundraising tools to raise money for a project, cause, or business venture.

7.   *Courses and webinars*: Offer online courses, webinars, or workshops related to your niche, and promote them on your Facebook page.

By utilizing these monetization methods, you can turn your Facebook page into a source of revenue and grow your business. It's important to be transparent and follow Facebook's policies regarding monetization and advertising.

Follow this link to Facebook's policies regarding monetization and advertising: https://www.facebook.com/policies/ads/

This page outlines Facebook's policies and guidelines for monetizing and advertising on its platform, including guidelines for sponsored content, advertising practices, and community standards. Review and follow these policies to ensure your page is in compliance and to avoid any potential issues or suspension of your account.

Conclusion

Starting a Facebook page for your business or personal brand can be a valuable tool for reaching a wider audience, building relationships, and promoting your brand. By creating engaging content, utilizing your personal profile, and finding effective monetization strategies, you can turn your Facebook page into a powerful tool for growing your business or personal brand. Building a successful Facebook page takes time, effort, and consistent engagement. By following best practices and staying up-to-date with changes in the platform, you can maximize your results and reach your goals on Facebook.

#25

Writing Articles

Writing for Income

An authority site is a website that is considered to be an expert in its niche or industry. These sites typically have high-quality content, a large following, and are considered trustworthy sources of information. Writing articles for authority sites can be a great way to establish yourself as an expert in your field and increase your visibility online. There can be earning potential through affiliate marketing, sponsored content, and advertising. Authority sites can also help to drive traffic to your own site and boost your search engine rankings. Writing for authority sites can be a great way to build your brand and grow your online presence.

Earning potential

Writing articles for authority sites is a great way to establish yourself as an expert in your field and increase your visibility online. Authority sites are websites that are considered to be experts in their niche or industry. These sites typically have high-quality content, a large following, and are considered trustworthy sources of information. As a result, writing for authority sites can help to establish credibility and trust with your target audience. There can be earning potential through affiliate marketing, sponsored content, and advertising. Authority sites can also help to drive traffic to your own site and boost your search engine rankings. Writing for authority sites can be a great way to build your brand and grow your online presence.

Skillset

To write articles for authority sites, there are several skills that are useful to have:

1. *Writing skills*: The ability to write clear, concise, and engaging text is essential for creating high-quality content that will be accepted by authority sites.

2. *Research skills*: The ability to research and fact-check information is important to ensure that the articles you write are accurate and credible.

3. *SEO skills*: Understanding the basics of search engine optimization (SEO) can help you to create content that is more likely to rank well in search engine results pages (SERPs).

4. *Niche knowledge*: Having a good understanding of the niche or industry that you are writing about will help you to create content that is both relevant and valuable to your target audience.

5. *Marketing skills*: Knowledge of digital marketing trends, techniques, and strategies will help you to promote your articles and reach a larger audience.

6. *Networking skills*: Building a network of contacts within your industry can be beneficial for finding new opportunities to write for authority sites and getting your work seen by more people.

The process of getting started

Here are some steps to get started with writing articles for authority sites:

1. *Research authority sites in your niche*: Look for websites that are considered to be experts in your field and have a large following. Make a list of these sites and take note of their content and style.

2. *Create a portfolio*: Gather samples of your best writing and create a portfolio that you can share with potential clients or editors.

3. *Network*: Reach out to other writers and industry professionals to build a network of contacts. You can also join online groups or communities related to your niche to connect with other writers and potential clients.

4. *Pitch your ideas*: Come up with article ideas that will be relevant and interesting to the readers of the authority sites you are targeting. Then, reach out to the editors or site owners with a pitch for your idea.

5. *Follow the guidelines*: Each authority site has its own set of guidelines for submitting content. Be sure to read and follow these guidelines to increase your chances of getting your work accepted.

6. *Be patient*: Be prepared for rejection. It may take time to build a relationship with an authority site and get your work accepted. Keep submitting your ideas and improve your skills.

7.   *Keep writing*: Keep writing and submitting your articles to different authority sites, this will increase your visibility and credibility in your niche.

Websites 1:

Here are a few examples of authority sites in different niches:

1.   **Forbes**: Forbes is a business and finance authority site that accepts articles on a wide range of topics, including entrepreneurship, leadership, and technology. The application process involves submitting a pitch to the Forbes contributor network and, if accepted, writing and submitting an article. Earnings potential can vary, but many contributors earn a flat fee for their articles.

2.   **HuffPost**: HuffPost (formerly known as The Huffington Post) is a news and opinion website that covers a wide range of topics. It has a large audience and a reputation for high-quality content. The application process involves submitting a pitch or an article to the editorial team.

3.   **Medium**: Medium is a platform for independent writers and bloggers to share their ideas and stories. Medium focuses on a wide range of topics, from personal development to technology. The application process is simple, you just need to create an account and start publishing your articles. A medium revenue-sharing program is based on how many views, claps, and shares an article receives.

4. **Entrepreneur**: Entrepreneur is a business authority site that covers topics such as startups, marketing, and leadership. The application process involves submitting a pitch to the Entrepreneur contributor network. Earnings potential can vary, but many contributors earn a flat fee for their articles.

5. **Inc**: Inc is a business and entrepreneurship website that covers a wide range of topics. It has a large audience and a reputation for high-quality content. To apply you will need to submit a pitch or an article to the editorial team.

The earning potential for writing articles for authority sites can vary greatly depending on the site, the niche, and the writer's experience. The application process for each site can also vary, so be sure to read the guidelines carefully and follow the instructions provided.

Websites 2:

All of the sites are well-established and considered authority sites in their respective niches. Here's an overview:

1. **Listverse**: Listverse is a website that publishes list-based articles on a wide range of topics. It is known for its unique and interesting content. https://listverse.com/

2. **The Penny Hoarder**: The Penny Hoarder is a personal finance website that provides tips and advice on saving money and earning extra income. https://www.thepennyhoarder.com/

3. **UX Booth**: UX Booth is a website that focuses on user experience design and research, with a variety of articles, tutorials, and case studies. https://www.uxbooth.com/

4. **Cracked**: Cracked is a humor website that publishes articles, videos, and other content with a comedic angle. https://www.cracked.com/

5. **Smashing Magazine**: Smashing Magazine is a website that focuses on web design and development, with articles, tutorials, and resources for web designers and developers. https://www.smashingmagazine.com/

6. **A List Apart**: A List Apart is a website that focuses on web design and development, with articles, tutorials, and resources for web designers and developers. https://alistapart.com/

7. **International Living**: International Living is a website that focuses on living and traveling abroad, with a variety of articles, resources, and guides for people interested in international travel and living. https://www.internationalliving.com/

8. **SitePoint**: SitePoint is a website that focuses on web design and development, with articles, tutorials, and resources for web designers and developers. https://www.sitepoint.com/

9. **Income Diary**: Income Diary is a website that focuses on making money online, with a variety of articles, tutorials, and resources for online entrepreneurs. https://www.incomediary.com/

10. **Great Escape Publishing**: Great Escape Publishing is a website that focuses on writing for travel magazines and websites, with a variety of articles, tutorials, and resources for travel writers. https://www.greatescapepublishing.com/

You can expect to find well-written, informative, and engaging content on these sites, and the earning potential can vary depending on the site and the niche. Some sites pay for contributions, others don't but can open up opportunities for the writer.

The websites' URLs and even the content of the sites may change over time, and some sites may not be accepting guest posts anymore. Also, make sure to read the guidelines and the terms of service before submitting your application.

Conclusion

Writing articles for authority sites can be a great way to establish yourself as an expert in your field and increase your visibility online. Authority sites are websites that are considered to be experts in their niche or industry, with high-quality content, a large following, and a reputation for being trustworthy sources of information. To be successful as a writer for authority sites, it is important to have good writing skills, research skills, SEO skills, knowledge of your niche, marketing skills, and networking skills. By following these tips and applying to different authority sites, you can increase your chances of getting your work accepted and grow your online presence. Remember that writing for authority sites can also be a great way to earn money through affiliate marketing, sponsored content, and advertising.

#26

Side Hustle: Poetry Writing

The Art of Online Writing

Poetry writing is the art of creating literary works that use language in a creative and evocative way to express emotions, and ideas, or tell a story. It is a form of self-expression and a way for writers to explore their thoughts, feelings, and experiences. In terms of earning potential, it can vary greatly depending on the poet's level of success and the outlets through which they publish and promote their work. Some poets may earn a living through publication royalties, grants, and speaking engagements, while others may supplement their income with other forms of writing or teaching. Becoming a professional poet and earning a living from it is a difficult task and many poets opt to do it as a hobby or passion rather than a profession.

Skillset

There are several skills that are important for poetry writing:

1.	*Creativity*: Poets need to be able to think outside the box and come up with unique and imaginative ideas to express in their work.

2.   *Writing skills*: Poets need to have a good command of the language and be able to use words effectively to convey their message.

3.   *Technical skills*: Poets have to be familiar with the technical aspects of poetry such as meter, rhyme, and verse forms.

4.   *Emotional intelligence*: Poets need to be able to tap into their emotions and those of others to create powerful and evocative works.

5.   *Critical thinking*: Poets have to be able to analyze their own work and that of others to improve their craft.

6.   *Research and reading*: Poets need to read extensively, both poetry and other literature, to expose themselves to different styles, techniques, and ideas.

7.   *Self-discipline*: Poets must set time aside to write, revise, and edit their work.

8.   *Marketing and Networking*: Poets should be able to promote their work and build connections in the poetry community, to increase the chances of getting their work published and reaching a wider audience.

Not all poets will possess all these skills, and some may excel in some areas more than others. Poetry writing is an art and, like any art, it requires practice, patience, and perseverance.

Websites

1.   **The Sun Magazine**: Pays $100-200 per poem.

https://thesunmagazine.org/submit/essays-fiction-poetry

2.   **Poetry Foundation**: Offers compensation at a rate of $10 per line, ensuring a minimum payment of $300 for accepted poetry submissions.

https://www.poetryfoundation.org/poetrymagazine/submit

3.   **AGNI**: Pays $20 per poem.

https://agnionline.bu.edu/submit/

4.   **Ploughshares**: Pays $25-40 per poem.

https://www.pshares.org/submit

5.   **The Nation**: Pays $150-200 per poem.

https://www.thenation.com/submission-guidelines/

6.   **The Threepenny Review**: Pays $200 per poem. https://www.threepennyreview.com/submissions.html

7.   **The Kenyon Review**: Pays $40 per poem.

https://kenyonreview.org/submit/

8.   **The Hudson Review**: Pays $30 per poem.

https://hudsonreview.com/about-us/submission-guidelines/

9.   **Rattle**: Pays $50 per poem.

https://rattle.submittable.com/submit

10. **Poetry Northwest**: Pays $25 per poem.

https://www.poetrynw.org/about/submissions-info/

11. **32 Poems**: Pays $40 per poem.

https://32poems.com/submission-guidelines/

12. **The New Criterion**: Pays $200 per poem.

https://newcriterion.com/bookstore?mode=poetrysubmissions

These rates can vary depending on the publication and the writer's level of experience. Some of the above-mentioned websites accept international submissions, others only from US-based writers, and some have specific themes or guidelines for submission, and it is important to check the submission guidelines before submitting your poetry. Submission fee is common in many poetry magazine/journals, and it's always a good idea to check for them before submitting your poetry.

Conclusion

Poetry writing is a form of self-expression that can be both challenging and rewarding. It requires a combination of creativity, writing skills, technical knowledge, emotional intelligence, and self-discipline. While earning a living solely from poetry can be difficult, there are many outlets for poets to submit and publish their work, some of which even offer payment for accepted submissions. As a poet, remember that the primary goal should always be to share your voice and your message with the world, and not to focus solely on the earning potential. Continue to nurture your writing, persist in submitting your work, and dedicate yourself to constantly refining your craft.

Epilogue

Dear friends, this is the end of our exploration of <u>Book 1: "26 Ways To Make Money Online"</u>. I would like to thank you for taking this journey with me. We've delved into a world of opportunities, learned about diverse strategies, and gained insights into the dynamic nature of the digital world.

But our adventure doesn't end here; in fact, it continues. In <u>Book 2</u>, I am presenting you with *27 additional ways* to make money online. As we wrap up this book, I'd like to invite you to take the next step on your online income journey. Both books cover a total of 53 chapters each outlining the details and opportunities of different methods to generate an online income.

In <u>Book 2</u>, titled <u>"27 Additional Ways To Make Money Online"</u>, we'll explore further the vast sea of online opportunities. You'll find more about exciting avenues such as *Amazon FBA*, where you can turn your entrepreneurial dreams into reality, and the world of *online tutoring*, where your knowledge can become a valuable asset. Discover how to make money *proofreading*, harness the power of *chatbots*, immerse yourself in the world of *mobile games*, explore the realm of *crowdfunding*, and master the art of *email marketing*.

But that's not all. In <u>Book 2</u>, we'll also explore the *art of blogging*, the potential of *translation services*, the magic of *WordPress plugins*, and so much more. Each chapter will be a gateway to a new realm of possibilities, and your potential for success will continue to expand.

If you're hungry for more knowledge, more strategies, and more opportunities to thrive in the online world, <u>"27 Additional</u>

Ways To Make Money Online" awaits you. I promise that the journey will provide you with exciting new knowledge and ideas.

Your determination and willingness to adapt will be your greatest allies as you continue to explore the boundless potential of the digital landscape. I look forward to seeing you in Book 2, where together, we will unlock the doors to even more possibilities.

Thank you for joining me on this adventure, and remember: The online world is filled with opportunities, and your potential for success is limited only by your willingness to explore, learn, and take action.

So, let's turn the page and continue this exciting journey together. I'll meet you in "27 Additional Ways To Make Money Online".

Happy exploring, and may your online endeavors be prosperous and fulfilling!

Kindly yours, The Author

More from this author:

MIDJOURNEY DIGEST: Make AI Art That Sells: List of Words 1000+ words to add to your prompts + Prompt Ideas

Available on Amazon and Kindle Unlimited

Mastering GPTs: A Comprehensive Guide To Creation, Utilization, And Monetization

Available on Amazon and Kindle Unlimited